HOLT SCIENCE & TECHNOLOGY

Electricity and Magnetism

HOLT, RINEHART AND WINSTON

A Harcourt Education Company

Orlando • **Austin** • New York • San Diego • Toronto • London

Acknowledgments

Contributing Authors

Andrew Champagne
Former Physics Teacher
Ashland, Massachusetts

Inclusion Specialist

Ellen McPeek Glisan
Special Needs Consultant
San Antonio, Texas

Safety Reviewer

Jack Gerlovich, Ph.D.
Associate Professor
School of Education
Drake University
Des Moines, Iowa

Academic Reviewers

David S. Hall, Ph.D.
*Assistant Professor
of Physics*
Department of Physics
Amherst College
Amherst, Massachusetts

William H. Ingham, Ph.D.
Professor of Physics
James Madison
University
Harrisonburg, Virginia

Mark Mattson, Ph.D.
Assistant Professor
Physics Department
James Madison
University
Harrisonburg, Virginia

Lab Testing

Paul Boyle
Science Teacher
Perry Heights Middle
School
Evansville, Indiana

Laura Fleet
Science Teacher
Alice B. Landrum Middle
School
Ponte Verde Beach,
Florida

Susan Gorman
Science Teacher
North Ridge Middle
School
North Richland Hills,
Texas

Tracy Jahn
Science Teacher
Berkshire Junior-Senior
High School
Canaan, New York

Alyson Mike
Science Teacher
East Valley Middle School
East Helena, Montana

Rodney A. Sandefur
Science Teacher
Naturita Middle School
Naturita, Colorado

Bert J. Sherwood
Science Teacher
Socorro Middle School
El Paso, Texas

David M. Sparks
Science Teacher
Redwater Junior High
School
Redwater, Texas

Teacher Reviewers

Diedre S. Adams
Physical Science Instructor
Science Department
West Vigo Middle School
West Terre Haute,
Indiana

Ronald W. Hudson
Science Teacher
Batchelor Middle School
Bloomington, Indiana

Denise Hulette
Teacher
Conway Middle School
Orlando, Florida

Bill Martin
Science Teacher
Southeast Middle School
Kernersville, North
Carolina

N Electricity and Magnetism

Safety First! x

CHAPTER 1 Introduction to Electricity 2

    SECTION 1 Electric Charge and Static Electricity 4
    SECTION 2 Electric Current and Electrical Energy 12
    SECTION 3 Electrical Calculations 20
    SECTION 4 Electric Circuits 24

Chapter Lab Skills Practice Circuitry 101 30
Chapter Review 32
Standardized Test Preparation 34
Science in Action 36

    LabBook **Skills Practice** Stop the Static Electricity! 100
    Model Making Potato Power 101

CHAPTER 2 Electromagnetism 38

    SECTION 1 Magnets and Magnetism 40
    SECTION 2 Magnetism from Electricity 48
    SECTION 3 Electricity from Magnetism 54

Chapter Lab Model Making Build a DC Motor 60
Chapter Review 62
Standardized Test Preparation 64
Science in Action 66

    LabBook **Skills Practice** Magnetic Mystery 102
    Skills Practice Electricity from Magnetism 103

CHAPTER **3** **Electronic Technology** **68**

SECTION 1 Electronic Devices 70
SECTION 2 Communication Technology 76
SECTION 3 Computers 84

Chapter Lab Skills Practice Sending Signals 92
Chapter Review 94
Standardized Test Preparation 96
Science in Action 98
LabBook **Model Making** Tune In! 104

Skills Development

PRE-READING ACTIVITY

FOLDNOTES
Layered Book 2
Booklet 68

Graphic Organizer
Comparison Table 38

START-UP ACTIVITY
Stick Together 3
Magnetic Attraction 39
Talking Long Distance 69

QUICK Lab
Detecting Charge 7
A Series of Circuits 26
A Parallel Lab 27
Model of Earth's Magnetic Field 45
Electromagnets 50
The Speed of a Simple
    Computer 85

SCHOOL to HOME
Saving Energy 23
TV Screen 81

READING STRATEGY
Brainstorming
Chapter 1 24
Discussion
Chapter 3 76
Paired Summarizing
Chapter 1 20
Chapter 2 54
Prediction Guide
Chapter 2 40
Chapter 3 84
Reading Organizer—Concept Map
Chapter 3 70
Reading Organizer—Outline
Chapter 1 4
Reading Organizer—Table
Chapter 1 12
Chapter 2 48

INTERNET ACTIVITY
CHAPTER 1
    Introduction to Electricity HP5ELEW
CHAPTER 2
    Electromagnetism HP5EMGW
CHAPTER 3
    Electronic Technology HP5ELTW

MATH PRACTICE
Transformers and Voltage 58
Computer Memory 87

MATH FOCUS
Using Ohm's Law 21
Power and Energy 22

Connection to . . .

Biology
Help for a Heart 15
Nervous Impulses 25
Animal Compasses 42

Environmental Science
Painting Cars 6

Geology
Seismograms 77

Social Studies
Benjamin Franklin 10
History of the Compass 46
ENIAC 86

Science in Action

Science Fiction
"There Will Come Soft Rains" 98

Science, Technology, and Society
Magnets in Medicine 66
Wearable Computers 98

Scientific Discoveries
Sprites and Elves 36

Weird Science
Electric Eels 36
Geomagnetic Storms 66

Careers
Pete Perez Electrician 37
Agnes Riley Computer Technician 99

People in Science
James Clerk Maxwell Magnetic Math 67

LabBook 100

Appendix 108
Reading Check Answers 109
Study Skills 110
SI Measurement 116
Temperature Scales 117
Measuring Skills 118
Scientific Methods 119
Making Charts and Graphs 121
Math Refresher 124
Physical Science Laws
  and Principles 128

Glossary 132

Spanish Glossary 134

Index 136

How to Use Your Textbook

Your Roadmap for Success with Holt Science and Technology

Reading Warm-Up

A Reading Warm-Up at the beginning of every section provides you with the section's objectives and key terms. The objectives tell you what you'll need to know after you finish reading the section.

Key terms are listed for each section. Learn the definitions of these terms because you will most likely be tested on them. Each key term is highlighted in the text and is defined at point of use and in the margin. You can also use the glossary to locate definitions quickly.

STUDY TIP Reread the objectives and the definitions to the key terms when studying for a test to be sure you know the material.

Get Organized

A Reading Strategy at the beginning of every section provides tips to help you organize and remember the information covered in the section. Keep a science notebook so that you are ready to take notes when your teacher reviews the material in class. Keep your assignments in this notebook so that you can review them when studying for the chapter test.

SECTION 3

Electrical Calculations

A German school teacher named Georg Ohm wondered how electric current, voltage, and resistance are related.

READING WARM-UP

Objectives
- Use Ohm's law to calculate voltage, current, and resistance.
- Calculate electric power.
- Determine the electrical energy used by a device.

Terms to Learn
electric power

READING STRATEGY

Paired Summarizing Read this section silently. In pairs, take turns summarizing the material. Stop to discuss ideas that seem confusing.

Connecting Current, Voltage, and Resistance

Ohm (1789–1854) studied the resistances of materials. He measured the current that resulted from different voltages applied to a piece of metal wire. The graph on the left in **Figure 1** is similar to the graph of his results.

Ohm's Law

Ohm found that the ratio of voltage (V) to current (I) is a constant for each material. This ratio is the resistance (R) of the material. When the voltage is expressed in volts (V) and the current is in amperes (A), the resistance is in ohms (Ω). The equation below is often called *Ohm's law* because of Ohm's work.

$$R = \frac{V}{I}, \text{ or } V = I \times R$$

As the resistance goes up, the current goes down. And as the resistance decreases, the current increases. The second graph in **Figure 1** shows this relationship. Notice that if you multiply the current and the resistance for any point, you get 16 V.

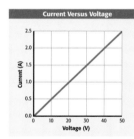
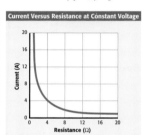

Figure 1 *The relationship between current and voltage is different from the relationship between current and resistance.*

490   Chapter 17   Introduction to Electricity

Be Resourceful—Use the Web

SCILINKS®

Internet Connect boxes in your textbook take you to resources that you can use for science projects, reports, and research papers. Go to scilinks.org, and type in the SciLinks code to get information on a topic.

go.hrw.com

Visit go.hrw.com

Find worksheets, **Current Science®** magazine articles online, and other materials that go with your textbook at **go.hrw.com**. Click on the textbook icon and the table of contents to see all of the resources for each chapter.

MATH FOCUS

Using Ohm's Law What is the voltage if the current is 2 A and the resistance is 12 Ω?

Step 1: Write the equation for voltage.

$$V = I \times R$$

Step 2: Replace the current and resistance with the measurements given in the problem, and solve.

$$V = 2 \text{ A} \times 12 \text{ }\Omega$$
$$V = 24 \text{ V}$$

Now It's Your Turn

1. Find the voltage if the current is 0.2 A and the resistance is 2 Ω.
2. The resistance of an object is 4 Ω. If the current in the object is 9 A, what voltage must be used?
3. An object has a resistance of 20 Ω. Calculate the voltage needed to produce a current of 0.5 A.

Electric Power

The rate at which electrical energy is changed into other forms of energy is **electric power**. The unit for power is the watt (W), and the symbol for power is the letter *P*. Electric power is expressed in watts when the voltage is in volts and the current is in amperes. Electric power is calculated by using the following equation:

power = voltage × current, or *P = V × I*

electric power the rate at which electrical energy is converted into other forms of energy

Watt: The Unit of Power

If you have ever changed a light bulb, you probably know about watts. Light bulbs, such as the ones in **Figure 2,** have labels such as "60 W," "75 W," or "120 W." As electrical energy is supplied to a light bulb, the light bulb glows. As power increases, the bulb burns brighter because more electrical energy is converted into light energy. The higher power rating of a 120 W bu ____ than a 60 W

Another watt (kW). C Kilowatts ar power, such house.

Reading C for electric p *Reading Checks*

How to Save Energy

Every appliance uses energy. But a fan, such as the one in **Figure 4,** could actually help you save energy. If you use a fan, you can run an air conditioner less. Replacing items that have high power ratings with items that have lower ratings is another way to save energy. Turning off lights when they are not in use will also help.

SCHOOL to HOME

Saving Energy

WRITING SKILL With a parent, identify the power rating for each light in your home and estimate how long each light is on during a day. In your **science journal,** determine how much electrical energy each light uses per day. Then, describe two ways to save energy with the lights.

ACTIVITY

Figure 4 *Using a fan to stay cool and using a small toaster instead of a larger toaster oven are ways to save energy.*

SECTION Review

Summary

- Ohm's law describes the relationship between current, resistance, and voltage.
- Electric power is the rate at which electrical energy is changed into other forms of energy.
- Electrical energy is electric power multiplied by time. It is usually expressed in kilowatt-hours.

Using Key Terms

1. In your own words, write a definition for the term *electric power.*

Understanding Key Ideas

2. Which of the following is Ohm's law?
   a. $E = P \times t$
   b. $I = V \times R$
   c. $P = V \times I$
   d. $V = I \times R$

3. Circuit A has twice the resistance of circuit B. The voltage is the same in each circuit. Which circuit has the higher current?

Math Skills

4. Use Ohm's law to find the voltage needed to make a current of 3 A in a resistance of 9 Ω.
5. How much electrical energy does a 40 W light bulb use if it is left on for 12 h?

Critical Thinking

6. **Applying Concepts** Explain why increasing the voltage applied to a wire can have the same effect on the current in the wire that decreasing the resistance of the wire does.

7. **Identifying Relationships** Using the equations in this section, develop an equation to find electrical energy from time, current, and resistance.

SCLINKS. **NSTA**

Developed and maintained by the National Science Teachers Association

For a variety of links related to this chapter, go to www.scilinks.org

Topic: Electrical Energy
SciLinks code: HSM0475

493

Use the Illustrations and Photos

Art shows complex ideas and processes. Learn to analyze the art so that you better understand the material you read in the text.

Tables and graphs display important information in an organized way to help you see relationships.

A picture is worth a thousand words. Look at the photographs to see relevant examples of science concepts that you are reading about.

Answer the Section Reviews

Section Reviews test your knowledge of the main points of the section. Critical Thinking items challenge you to think about the material in greater depth and to find connections that you infer from the text.

STUDY TIP When you can't answer a question, reread the section. The answer is usually there.

Do Your Homework

Your teacher may assign worksheets to help you understand and remember the material in the chapter.

STUDY TIP Don't try to answer the questions without reading the text and reviewing your class notes. A little preparation up front will make your homework assignments a lot easier. Answering the items in the Chapter Review will help prepare you for the chapter test.

Holt Online Learning

Visit Holt Online Learning

If your teacher gives you a special password to log onto the Holt Online Learning site, you'll find your complete textbook on the Web. In addition, you'll find some great learning tools and practice quizzes. You'll be able to see how well you know the material from your textbook.

CNN student News™

Visit CNN Student News

You'll find up-to-date events in science at cnnstudentnews.com.

SAFETY FIRST!

Exploring, inventing, and investigating are essential to the study of science. However, these activities can also be dangerous. To make sure that your experiments and explorations are safe, you must be aware of a variety of safety guidelines. You have probably heard of the saying, "It is better to be safe than sorry." This is particularly true in a science classroom where experiments and explorations are being performed. Being uninformed and careless can result in serious injuries. Don't take chances with your own safety or with anyone else's.

The following pages describe important guidelines for staying safe in the science classroom. Your teacher may also have safety guidelines and tips that are specific to your classroom and laboratory. Take the time to be safe.

Safety Rules!

Start Out Right

Always get your teacher's permission before attempting any laboratory exploration. Read the procedures carefully, and pay particular attention to safety information and caution statements. If you are unsure about what a safety symbol means, look it up or ask your teacher. You cannot be too careful when it comes to safety. If an accident does occur, inform your teacher immediately regardless of how minor you think the accident is.

If you are instructed to note the odor of a substance, wave the fumes toward your nose with your hand. Never put your nose close to the source.

Safety Symbols

All of the experiments and investigations in this book and their related worksheets include important safety symbols to alert you to particular safety concerns. Become familiar with these symbols so that when you see them, you will know what they mean and what to do. It is important that you read this entire safety section to learn about specific dangers in the laboratory.

Eye protection

Clothing protection

Hand safety

Heating safety

Electric safety

Chemical safety

Animal safety

Sharp object

Plant safety

x

Eye Safety

Wear safety goggles when working around chemicals, acids, bases, or any type of flame or heating device. Wear safety goggles any time there is even the slightest chance that harm could come to your eyes. If any substance gets into your eyes, notify your teacher immediately and flush your eyes with running water for at least 15 minutes. Treat any unknown chemical as if it were a dangerous chemical. Never look directly into the sun. Doing so could cause permanent blindness.

Avoid wearing contact lenses in a laboratory situation. Even if you are wearing safety goggles, chemicals can get between the contact lenses and your eyes. If your doctor requires that you wear contact lenses instead of glasses, wear eye-cup safety goggles in the lab.

Safety Equipment

Know the locations of the nearest fire alarms and any other safety equipment, such as fire blankets and eyewash fountains, as identified by your teacher, and know the procedures for using the equipment.

Neatness

Keep your work area free of all unnecessary books and papers. Tie back long hair, and secure loose sleeves or other loose articles of clothing, such as ties and bows. Remove dangling jewelry. Don't wear open-toed shoes or sandals in the laboratory. Never eat, drink, or apply cosmetics in a laboratory setting. Food, drink, and cosmetics can easily become contaminated with dangerous materials.

Certain hair products (such as aerosol hair spray) are flammable and should not be worn while working near an open flame. Avoid wearing hair spray or hair gel on lab days.

Sharp/Pointed Objects

Use knives and other sharp instruments with extreme care. Never cut objects while holding them in your hands. Place objects on a suitable work surface for cutting.

Be extra careful when using any glassware. When adding a heavy object to a graduated cylinder, tilt the cylinder so that the object slides slowly to the bottom.

Heat ⬦ ⬦ ⬦

Wear safety goggles when using a heating device or a flame. Whenever possible, use an electric hot plate as a heat source instead of using an open flame. When heating materials in a test tube, always angle the test tube away from yourself and others. To avoid burns, wear heat-resistant gloves whenever instructed to do so.

Electricity ⬦

Be careful with electrical cords. When using a microscope with a lamp, do not place the cord where it could trip someone. Do not let cords hang over a table edge in a way that could cause equipment to fall if the cord is accidentally pulled. Do not use equipment with damaged cords. Be sure that your hands are dry and that the electrical equipment is in the "off" position before plugging it in. Turn off and unplug electrical equipment when you are finished.

Chemicals ⬦ ⬦ ⬦ ⬦

Wear safety goggles when handling any potentially dangerous chemicals, acids, or bases. If a chemical is unknown, handle it as you would a dangerous chemical. Wear an apron and protective gloves when you work with acids or bases or whenever you are told to do so. If a spill gets on your skin or clothing, rinse it off immediately with water for at least 5 minutes while calling to your teacher.

Never mix chemicals unless your teacher tells you to do so. Never taste, touch, or smell chemicals unless you are specifically directed to do so. Before working with a flammable liquid or gas, check for the presence of any source of flame, spark, or heat.

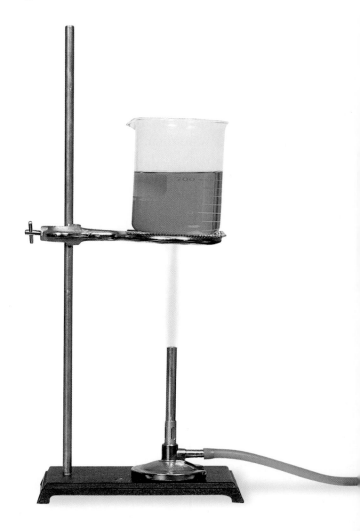

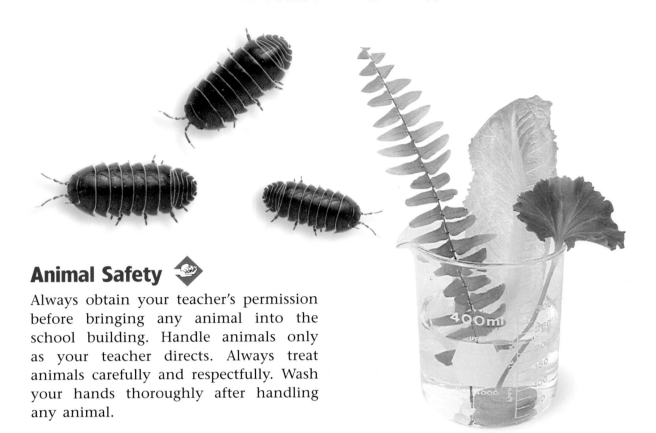

Animal Safety

Always obtain your teacher's permission before bringing any animal into the school building. Handle animals only as your teacher directs. Always treat animals carefully and respectfully. Wash your hands thoroughly after handling any animal.

Plant Safety

Do not eat any part of a plant or plant seed used in the laboratory. Wash your hands thoroughly after handling any part of a plant. When in nature, do not pick any wild plants unless your teacher instructs you to do so.

Glassware

Examine all glassware before use. Be sure that glassware is clean and free of chips and cracks. Report damaged glassware to your teacher. Glass containers used for heating should be made of heat-resistant glass.

1

Introduction to Electricity

SECTION **1** **Electric Charge
and Static Electricity** 4

SECTION **2** **Electric Current and
Electrical Energy**....... 12

SECTION **3** **Electrical Calculations** 20

SECTION **4** **Electric Circuits** 24

Chapter Lab 30
Chapter Review 32
Standardized Test Preparation 34
Science in Action................. 36

About the  PHOTO

This incredible light display is not an indoor lightning storm, but it's close! When scientists at the Sandia National Laboratory fire this fusion device, a huge number of electrons move across the room and make giant sparks.

PRE-READING ACTIVITY

 **Layered Book** Before you read the chapter, create the FoldNote entitled "Layered Book" described in the **Study Skills** section of the Appendix. Label the tabs of the layered book with "Charge," "Current," "Voltage," and "Resistance." As you read the chapter, write information you learn about each category under the appropriate tab.

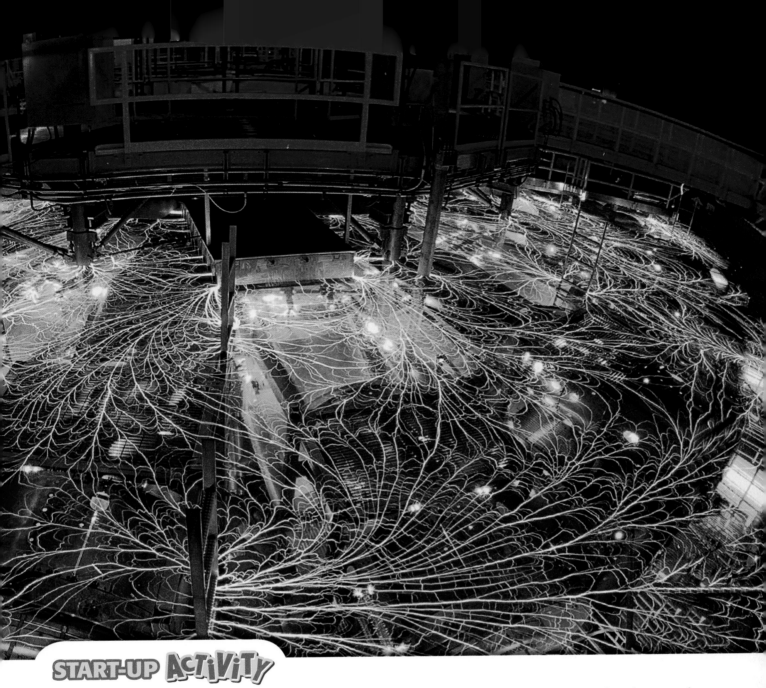

START-UP ACTIVITY

Stick Together

In this activity, you will see how a pair of electrically charged objects interact.

Procedure

1. Take **two strips of cellophane tape.** Each strip should be 20 cm long. Fold over a small part of the end of each strip to form a tab.

2. Hold each piece of tape by its tab. Bring the two pieces of tape close together, but do not let them touch. Record your observations.

3. Tape one of the strips to your lab table. Tape the second strip on top of the first strip.

4. Pull the strips of tape off the table together.

5. Quickly pull the strips apart. Bring the two pieces of tape close together, but do not let them touch. Record your observations.

Analysis

1. Compare how the pieces of tape behaved when you first brought them together with how they behaved after you pulled the pieces apart.

2. As you pulled the pieces of tape apart, electrons from one piece of tape moved onto the other piece of tape. Describe the charge on each piece of tape after you pulled the two pieces apart.

3. From your observations, draw a conclusion about how objects having the charges that you described behave toward one another.

Electric Charge and Static Electricity

Have you ever reached out to open a door and received a shock from the doorknob? Why did that happen?

On dry days, you might get a shock when you open a door, put on a sweater, or touch another person. These shocks come from static electricity. To understand static electricity, you need to learn about atoms and charge.

Electric Charge

All matter is made up of very small particles called *atoms*. Atoms are made of even smaller particles called protons, neutrons, and electrons, which are shown in **Figure 1.** How do these particles differ? For one thing, protons and electrons are charged particles, and neutrons are not.

✓ **Reading Check** What are the two types of charged particles in atoms? (*See the Appendix for answers to Reading Checks.*)

Charges Exert Forces

Charge is a physical property. An object can have a positive charge, a negative charge, or no charge. Charge is best understood by learning how charged objects interact. Charged objects exert a force—a push or a pull—on other charged objects. The **law of electric charges** states that like charges repel, or push away, and opposite charges attract. **Figure 2** illustrates this law.

READING WARM-UP

Objectives

- Describe how charged objects interact by using the law of electric charges.
- Describe three ways in which an object can become charged.
- Compare conductors with insulators.
- Give two examples of static electricity and electric discharge.

Terms to Learn

law of electric charges
electric force
electric field
electrical conductor
electrical insulator
static electricity
electric discharge

READING STRATEGY

Reading Organizer As you read this section, create an outline of the section. Use the headings from the section in your outline.

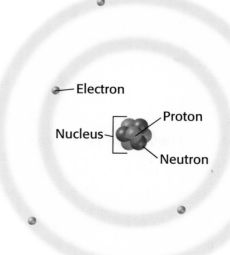

Figure 1 *Protons and neutrons make up the center of the atom, the nucleus. Electrons are found outside the nucleus.*

Electron

Proton

Nucleus

Neutron

Figure 2 The Law of Electric Charges

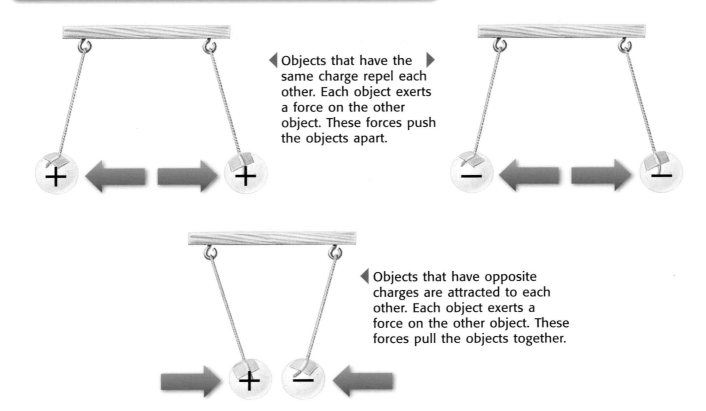

Objects that have the same charge repel each other. Each object exerts a force on the other object. These forces push the objects apart.

Objects that have opposite charges are attracted to each other. Each object exerts a force on the other object. These forces pull the objects together.

The Force Between Protons and Electrons

Protons are positively charged. Electrons are negatively charged. Because protons and electrons have opposite charges, they are attracted to each other. Without this attraction, electrons would fly away from the nucleus of an atom.

The Electric Force and the Electric Field

The force between charged objects is an **electric force.** The size of the electric force depends on two things. The first thing is the amount of each charge. The greater the charges are, the greater the electric force is. The other thing that determines the size of the electric force is the distance between the charges. The closer together the charges are, the greater the electric force is.

Charged things are affected by electric force because charged things have an electric field around them. An **electric field** is the region around a charged object in which an electric force is exerted on another charged object. A charged object in the electric field of another charged object is attracted or repelled by the electric force acting on it.

law of electric charges the law that states that like charges repel and opposite charges attract

electric force the force of attraction or repulsion on a charged particle that is due to an electric field

electric field the space around a charged object that causes another charged object to experience an electric force

Charge It!

Atoms have equal numbers of protons and electrons. Because an atom's positive and negative charges cancel each other out, atoms do not have a charge. So, how can anything made of atoms be charged? An object becomes positively charged when it loses electrons. An object becomes negatively charged when it gains electrons. Objects can become charged by friction, conduction, and induction, as shown in **Figure 3.**

✓ **Reading Check** What are three ways of charging an object?

Friction

Charging by *friction* happens when electrons are "wiped" from one object onto another. If you use a cloth to rub a plastic ruler, electrons move from the cloth to the ruler. The ruler gains electrons and becomes negatively charged. At the same time, the cloth loses electrons and becomes positively charged.

Conduction

Charging by *conduction* happens when electrons move from one object to another by direct contact. Suppose you touch an uncharged piece of metal with a positively charged glass rod. Electrons from the metal will move to the glass rod. The metal loses electrons and becomes positively charged.

**CONNECTION TO
Environmental Science**

WRITING SKILL **Painting Cars** Research how charge and electric force are used by car makers to paint cars. Then, in your **science journal,** write a one-page report describing the process and explaining how the use of charge to paint cars helps protect the environment.

Figure 3 Three Ways to Charge an Object

Friction	Conduction	Induction

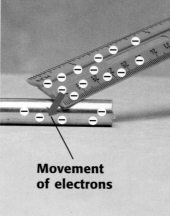

Movement of electrons

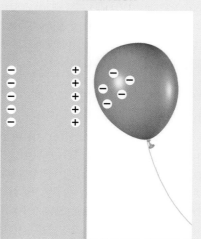

The friction of rubbing a balloon on your hair causes electrons to move from your hair to the balloon. Your hair and the balloon become oppositely charged and attract each other.

When a negatively charged plastic ruler touches an uncharged metal rod, the electrons in the ruler travel to the rod. The rod becomes negatively charged by conduction.

A negatively charged balloon makes a small section of a metal beam have a positive charge through induction. Electrons in the metal are repelled by and move away from the balloon.

Induction

Charging by *induction* happens when charges in an uncharged metal object are rearranged without direct contact with a charged object. Suppose you hold a metal object near a positively charged object. The electrons in the metal are attracted to and move toward the positively charged object. This movement causes (or induces) an area of negative charge on the surface of the metal.

Conservation of Charge

When you charge something by any method, no charges are created or destroyed. The numbers of electrons and protons stay the same. Electrons simply move from one atom to another, which makes areas that have different charges. Because charges are not created or destroyed, charge is said to be conserved.

Detecting Charge

You can use a device called an *electroscope* to see if something is charged. An electroscope is a glass flask that has a metal rod in its rubber stopper. Two metal leaves are attached to the bottom of the rod. When the electroscope is not charged, the leaves hang straight down. When the electroscope is charged, the leaves repel each other, or spread apart.

Figure 4 shows a negatively charged ruler touching the rod of an electroscope. Electrons move from the ruler to the electroscope. The leaves become negatively charged and repel each other. If something that is positively charged touches the neutral rod, electrons move off the electroscope. Then, the leaves become positively charged and repel each other. An electroscope can show that an object is charged. However, it cannot show whether the charge is positive or negative.

✔ **Reading Check** What can you do with an electroscope?

Figure 4 *When an electroscope is charged, the metal leaves have the same charge and repel each other.*

Detecting Charge

1. Use **scissors** to cut **two strips of aluminum foil** that are 1 cm × 4 cm each.
2. Bend a **paper clip** to make a hook. (The clip will look like an upside-down question mark.)
3. Push the end of the hook through the middle of an **index card,** and tape the hook so that it hangs straight down from the card.
4. Lay the two foil strips on top of one another, and hang them on the hook by gently pushing the hook through them.
5. Lay the card over the top of a **glass jar.**
6. Bring **various charged objects** near the top of the paper-clip hook, and observe what happens. Explain your observations.

Moving Charges

Look at **Figure 5.** Have you ever noticed that electrical cords are often made from metal and plastic? Different materials are used because electric charges move through some materials more easily than they move through others. Most materials are either conductors or insulators based on how easily charges move in them.

Conductors

An **electrical conductor** is a material in which charges can move easily. Most metals are good conductors because some of their electrons are free to move. Conductors are used to make wires. For example, a lamp cord has metal wire and metal prongs. Copper, aluminum, and mercury are good conductors.

Insulators

An **electrical insulator** is a material in which charges cannot move easily. Insulators do not conduct charges very well because their electrons cannot flow freely. The electrons are tightly held in the atoms of the insulator. The insulating material in a lamp cord stops charges from leaving the wire and protects you from electric shock. Plastic, rubber, glass, wood, and air are good insulators.

Figure 5 *These jumper cables are made of metal, which carries electric charges, and plastic, which keeps the charges away from your hands.*

electrical conductor a material in which charges can move freely

electrical insulator a material in which charges cannot move freely

static electricity electric charge at rest; generally produced by friction or induction

Static Electricity

After you take your clothes out of the dryer, they sometimes are stuck together. They stick together because of static electricity. **Static electricity** is the electric charge at rest on an object.

When something is *static,* it is not moving. The charges of static electricity do not move away from the object that they are in. So, the object keeps its charge. Your clothes are charged by friction as they rub against each other inside a dryer. As the clothes tumble, negative charges are lost by some clothes and build up on other clothes. When the dryer stops, the transfer of charges also stops. And because clothing is an insulator, the built-up electric charges stay on each piece of clothing. The result of this buildup of charges is static cling.

Electric Discharge

Charges that build up as static electricity on an object eventually leave the object. The loss of static electricity as charges move off an object is called **electric discharge.** Sometimes, electric discharge happens slowly. For example, clothes stuck together by static electricity will eventually separate on their own. Over time, their electric charges move to water molecules in the air.

Sometimes, electric discharge happens quickly. It may happen with a flash of light, a shock, or a crackling noise. For example, when you wear rubber-soled shoes and walk on carpet, negative charges build up on your body. When you reach out for a metal doorknob, the negative charges on your body can jump to the doorknob. The electric discharge happens quickly, and you feel a small shock.

One of the most dramatic examples of electric discharge is lightning. How does lightning form through a buildup of static electricity? **Figure 6** shows the answer.

electric discharge the release of electricity stored in a source

✔️ **Reading Check** What is electric discharge?

Figure 6 How Lightning Forms

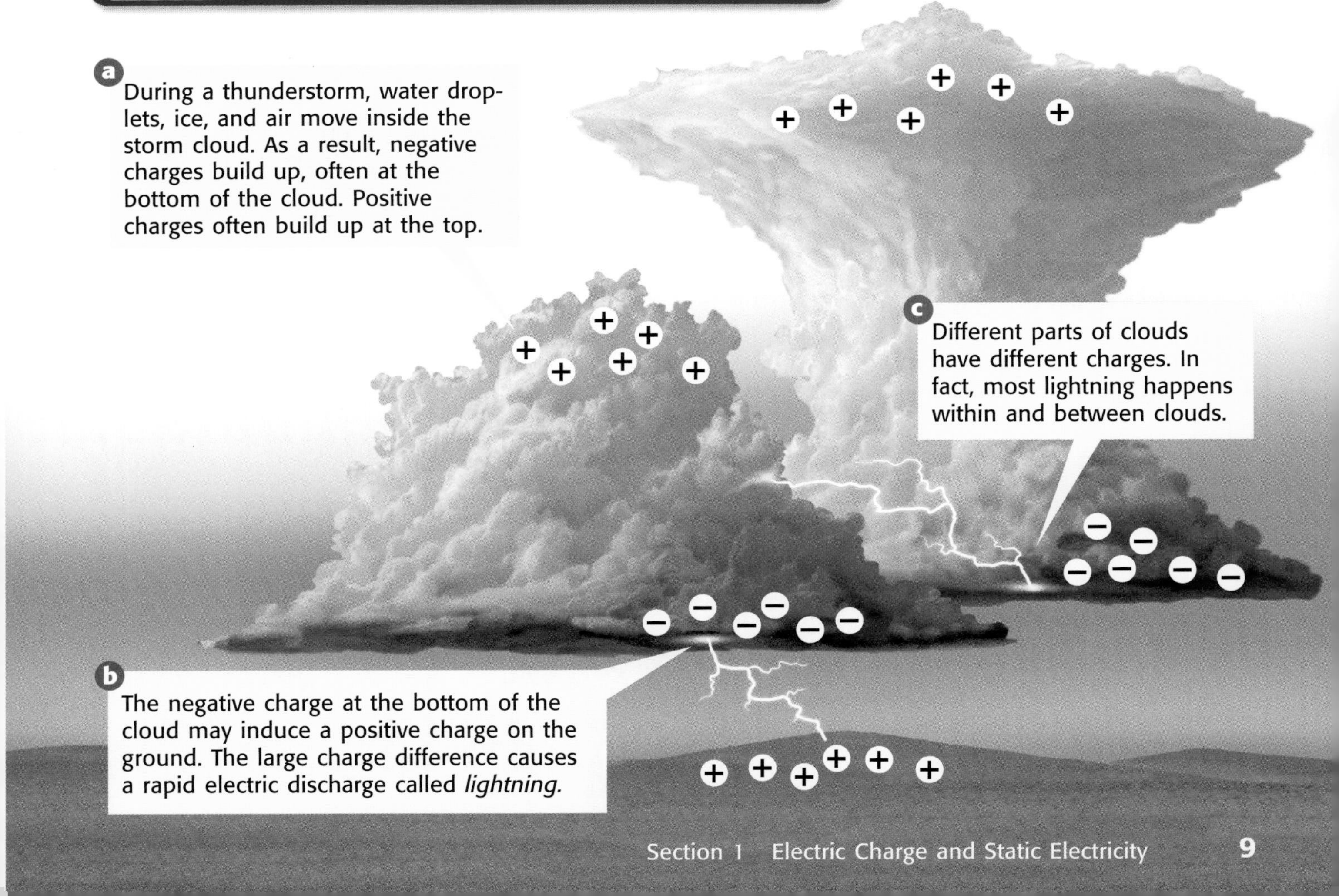

a During a thunderstorm, water droplets, ice, and air move inside the storm cloud. As a result, negative charges build up, often at the bottom of the cloud. Positive charges often build up at the top.

c Different parts of clouds have different charges. In fact, most lightning happens within and between clouds.

b The negative charge at the bottom of the cloud may induce a positive charge on the ground. The large charge difference causes a rapid electric discharge called *lightning.*

Lightning Dangers

Lightning usually strikes the highest point in a charged area because that point provides the shortest path for the charges to reach the ground. Anything that sticks up or out in an area can provide a path for lightning. Trees and people in open areas are at risk of being struck by lightning. For this reason, it is particularly dangerous to be at the beach or on a golf course during a lightning storm. Even standing under a tree during a storm is dangerous. The charges from lightning striking a tree can jump to your body.

Reading Check Why is it dangerous to be outside in an open area during a storm?

Lightning Rods

A lightning rod is a pointed rod connected to the ground by a wire. Lightning rods are often mounted so that they are the tallest point on a building, as shown in **Figure 7.** Objects, such as a lightning rod, that are joined to Earth by a conductor, such as a wire, are *grounded*. Any object that is grounded provides a path for electric charges to move to Earth. Because Earth is so large, it can give up or absorb charges without being damaged. When lightning strikes a lightning rod, the electric charges are carried safely to Earth through the rod's wire. By directing the charge to Earth, the rods prevent lightning from damaging buildings.

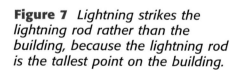

Figure 7 *Lightning strikes the lightning rod rather than the building, because the lightning rod is the tallest point on the building.*

Summary

- The law of electric charges states that like charges repel and opposite charges attract.
- The size of the electric force between two objects depends on the size of the charges exerting the force and the distance between the objects.
- Charged objects exert a force on each other and can cause each other to move.
- Objects become charged when they gain or lose electrons.

- Objects may become charged by friction, conduction, or induction.
- Charges are not created or destroyed and are said to be conserved.
- Charges move easily in conductors but do not move easily in insulators.
- Static electricity is the buildup of electric charges on an object. It is lost through electric discharge.

Using Key Terms

For each pair of terms, explain how the meanings of the terms differ.

1. *static electricity* and *electric discharge*
2. *electric force* and *electric field*
3. *electrical conductor* and *electrical insulator*

Understanding Key Ideas

4. Which of the following is an insulator?
   a. copper
   b. rubber
   c. aluminum
   d. iron

5. Compare the three methods of charging.

6. What does the law of electric charges say about two objects that are positively charged?

7. Give two examples of static electricity.

8. List two examples of electric discharge.

Critical Thinking

9. **Analyzing Processes** Imagine that you touch the top of an electroscope with an object. The metal leaves spread apart. Can you determine whether the charge is positive or negative? Explain your answer.

10. **Applying Concepts** Why is it important to touch a charged object to the metal rod of an electroscope and not to the rubber stopper?

Interpreting Graphics

The photograph below shows two charged balloons. Use the photograph below to answer the questions that follow.

11. Do the balloons have the same charge or opposite charges? Explain your answer.

12. How would the photograph look if each balloon were given the charge opposite to the charge it has now? Explain your answer.

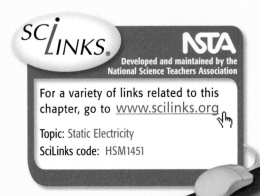

Electric Current and Electrical Energy

You might not realize that when you watch TV, use a computer, or even turn on a light bulb, you depend on moving charges for the electrical energy that you need.

Electrical energy is the energy of electric charges. In most of the things that use electrical energy, the electric charges flow through wires. As you read on, you will learn more about how this flow of charges—called *electric current*—is made and how it is controlled in the things that you use every day.

Electric Current

An **electric current** is the rate at which charges pass a given point. The higher the current is, the greater the number of charges that pass the point each second. Electric current is expressed in units called *amperes* (AM PIRZ), which is often shortened to *amps*. The symbol for *ampere* is A. And in equations, the symbol for current is the letter I.

✓ *Reading Check* **What is the unit of measurement for electric current?** (*See the Appendix for answers to Reading Checks.*)

Making Charges Move

When you flip the switch on a flashlight, the light comes on instantly. But do charges in the battery instantly reach the bulb? No, they don't. When you flip the switch, an electric field is set up in the wire at the speed of light. And the electric field causes the free electrons in the wire to move. The energy of each electron is transferred instantly to the next electron, as shown in **Figure 1**.

READING WARM-UP

Objectives

● Describe electric current.
● Describe voltage and its relationship to electric current.
● Describe resistance and its relationship to electric current.
● Explain how a cell generates electrical energy.
● Describe how thermocouples and photocells generate electrical energy.

Terms to Learn

electric current
voltage
resistance
cell
thermocouple
photocell

READING STRATEGY

Reading Organizer As you read this section, make a table comparing electric current, voltage, and resistance.

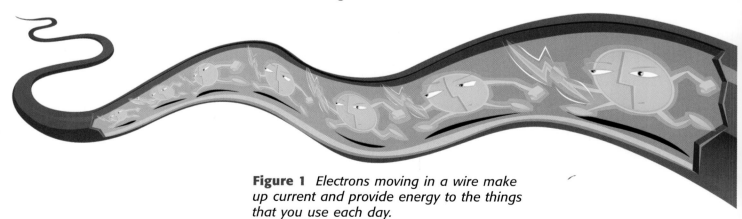

Figure 1 *Electrons moving in a wire make up current and provide energy to the things that you use each day.*

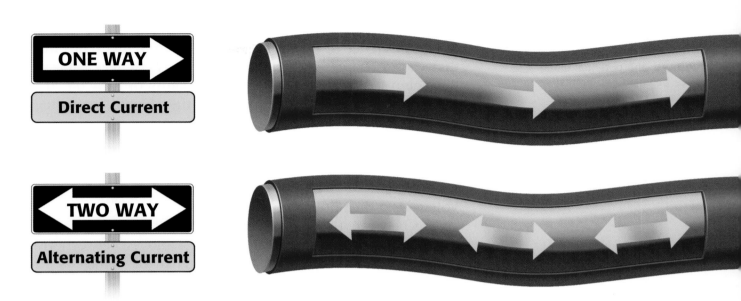

ONE WAY
Direct Current

TWO WAY
Alternating Current

Figure 2 *Charges move in one direction in DC, but charges continually change direction in AC.*

Commanding Electrons to Move

This electric field is created so quickly that all electrons start moving through the wire at the same instant. Think of the electric field as a command to the electrons to charge ahead. The light comes on instantly because all of the electrons obey this command at the same time. So, the current that lights the bulb is established very quickly even though each electron moves quite slowly. In fact, a single electron may take more than an hour to travel 1 m through a wire.

electric current the rate at which charges pass through a given point; measured in amperes

AC and DC

There are two kinds of electric current—direct current (DC) and alternating current (AC). Look at **Figure 2.** In direct current, the charges always flow in the same direction. In alternating current, the charges continually shift from flowing in one direction to flowing in the reverse direction.

The electric current from the batteries used in a camera is DC. The electric current from outlets in your home is AC. In the United States, the alternating current changes directions 120 times each second, or has 60 cycles each second.

Both kinds of current can give you electrical energy. For example, if you connect a flashlight bulb to a battery, the light bulb will light. And you can light a household light bulb by putting it in a lamp and turning the lamp on.

✓ **Reading Check** What are two kinds of electric current?

Voltage

If you are on a bike at the top of a hill, you know that you can roll down to the bottom. You can roll down the hill because of the difference in height between the two points. The "hill" that causes charges in a circuit to move is voltage. **Voltage** is the potential difference between two points in a circuit. It is expressed in volts (V). In equations, the symbol for voltage is the letter V.

voltage the potential difference between two points; measured in volts

✓ **Reading Check** What is the unit of measurement for voltage?

Voltage and Energy

Voltage is a measure of how much work is needed to move a charge between two points. You can think of voltage as the amount of energy released as a charge moves between two points in the path of a current. The higher the voltage is, the more energy is released per charge.

Voltage and Electric Current

As long as there is a voltage between two points on a wire, charges will flow in the wire. The size of the current depends on the voltage. The greater the voltage is, the greater the current is. A greater current means that more charges move in the wire each second. A large current is needed to start a car. So, the battery in a car has a fairly high voltage of 12 V. **Figure 3** shows batteries that have a number of different voltages. If you have a device that uses direct current, one of these batteries might help.

Figure 3 *Batteries are made with various voltages for use in many different devices.*

12 V

6 V

1.5 V

9 V

Figure 4 *An electric eel can create a voltage of more than 600 V!*

Varying Nature of Voltage

Things that run on batteries usually need a low voltage. For example, a portable radio might need only 3 V. Compare the voltage of such a radio with the voltage created by the eel in **Figure 4.** Most devices in your home use alternating current from an outlet. In the United States, electrical outlets usually supply AC at 120 V. So, most electrical devices, such as televisions, toasters, and alarm clocks, are made to run on 120 V.

Resistance

Resistance is another factor that determines the amount of current in a wire. **Resistance** is the opposition to the flow of electric charge. Resistance is expressed in ohms (Ω, the Greek letter *omega*). In equations, the symbol for resistance is the letter R.

You can think of resistance as "electrical friction." The higher the resistance of a material is, the lower the current in the material is. So, if the voltage doesn't change, as resistance goes up, current goes down. An object's resistance depends on the object's material, thickness, length, and temperature.

Resistance and Material

Good conductors, such as copper, have low resistance. Poor conductors, such as iron, have higher resistance. The resistance of insulators is so high that electric charges cannot flow in them. Materials with low resistance, such as copper, are used to make wires. But materials with high resistance are also helpful. For example, the high resistance of the filament in a light bulb causes the light bulb to heat up and give off light.

CONNECTION TO Biology

Help for a Heart Pacemaker cells in the heart produce low electric currents at regular intervals to make the heart beat. During a heart attack, pacemaker cells do not work together, and the heart beats irregularly. Research how doctors sometimes "jump start" the heart during a heart attack. Make a poster to share your findings.

ACTiViTY

resistance in physical science, the opposition presented to the current by a material or device

Figure 5 A Model of Resistance

A thick pipe has less resistance than a thin pipe does because there are more spaces between pieces of gravel in a thick pipe for water to flow through.

A short pipe has less resistance than a long pipe does because the water in a short pipe does not have to work its way around as many pieces of gravel.

Resistance, Thickness, and Length

To understand how the thickness and length of a wire affect the wire's resistance, look at the model in **Figure 5.** The pipe filled with gravel represents a wire. The water flowing through the pipe represents electric charges.

Resistance and Temperature

Resistance also depends on temperature. In general, the resistance of metals increases as temperature rises. The atoms vibrate faster at higher temperatures and get in the way of the flowing electric charges. If you cool certain materials to a very low temperature, resistance will drop to 0 Ω. Materials in this state are called *superconductors*. A small superconductor is shown in **Figure 6.** Very little energy is wasted when electric charges move in a superconductor. However, a large amount of energy is needed to cool them. Scientists are studying how superconductors can be used to store and transmit energy.

Figure 6 *One interesting property of superconductors is that they repel magnets. The superconductor in this photo is repelling the magnet so strongly that the magnet is floating.*

Figure 7 How a Cell Works

Flow

a A chemical reaction with the electrolyte leaves extra electrons on one electrode. This electrode is made of zinc.

b A different chemical reaction causes electrons to be pulled off the other electrode. In this cell, this electrode is made of copper.

c If the electrodes are connected by a wire, electrons flow through the wire and ions move in the electrolyte. The moving charges make an electric current.

Generating Electrical Energy

You know that energy cannot be created or destroyed. It can only be changed into other kinds of energy. Many things change different kinds of energy into electrical energy. For example, generators convert mechanical energy into electrical energy. **Cells** change chemical or radiant energy into electrical energy. Batteries are made of one or more cells.

cell in electricity, a device that produces an electric current by converting chemical or radiant energy into electrical energy

Parts of a Cell

A cell, such as the one in **Figure 7,** contains a mixture of chemicals called an *electrolyte* (ee LEK troh LIET). Electrolytes allow charges to flow. Every cell also has a pair of electrodes made from conducting materials. An *electrode* (ee LEK TROHD) is the part of a cell through which charges enter or exit. Chemical changes between the electrolyte and the electrodes convert chemical energy into electrical energy.

Kinds of Cells

Two kinds of cells are wet cells and dry cells. Wet cells, such as the one in **Figure 7,** have liquid electrolytes. A car battery is made of several wet cells that use sulfuric acid as the electrolyte. You can make your own wet cell by poking strips of zinc and copper into a lemon. When the metal strips are connected, enough electrical energy is generated to run a small clock, as shown in **Figure 8.** Dry cells work in a similar way. But the electrolytes in dry cells are solid or pastelike. The cells used in small radios and flashlights are types of dry cells.

Figure 8 *This cell uses the juice of a lemon as an electrolyte and uses strips of zinc and copper as electrodes.*

✓ **Reading Check** What are two kinds of cells?

Thermocouples

Thermal energy can be converted into electrical energy by a **thermocouple.** A simple thermocouple, shown in **Figure 9,** is made by joining wires of two different metals into a loop. The temperature difference within the loop causes charges to flow through the loop. The greater the temperature difference is, the greater the current is. Thermocouples usually do not generate much energy. But they are useful for monitoring the temperatures of car engines, furnaces, and ovens.

Photocells

If you look at a solar-powered calculator, you will see a dark strip called a *solar panel*. This panel is made of several photocells. A **photocell** converts light energy into electrical energy. How do photocells work? Most photocells contain silicon atoms. As long as light shines on the photocell, electrons gain enough energy to move between atoms. The electrons are then able to move through a wire to provide electrical energy to power a device, such as a calculator.

In larger panels, photocells can provide energy to buildings and cars. Large panels of photocells are even used on satellites. By changing light energy from the sun into electrical energy, the photocells provide energy to the many devices on the satellite to keep the devices working.

Reading Check What device converts light energy into electrical energy?

For another activity related to this chapter, go to **go.hrw.com** and type in the keyword **HP5ELEW.**

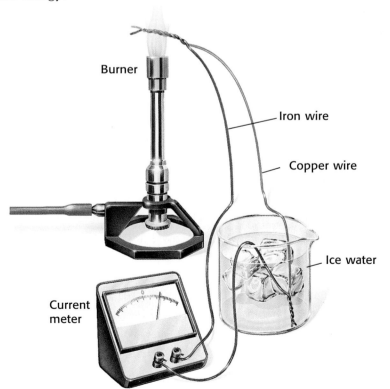

Burner

Iron wire

Copper wire

Ice water

Current meter

Figure 9 *In a simple thermocouple, one section of the loop is heated and one section is cooled.*

SECTION Review

Summary

- Electric current is the rate at which charges pass a given point.
- An electric current can be made when there is a potential difference between two points.
- As voltage, or potential difference increases, current increases.
- An object's resistance varies depending on the object's material, thickness, length, and temperature. As resistance increases, current decreases.
- Cells and batteries convert chemical energy or radiant energy into electrical energy.
- Thermocouples and photocells are devices used to generate electrical energy.

Using Key Terms

Complete each of the following sentences by choosing the correct term from the word bank.

voltage	electric current
resistance	cell

1. The rate at which charges pass a point is a(n) ___.

2. The opposition to the flow of charge is ___.

3. Another term for *potential difference* is ___.

4. A device that changes chemical energy into electrical energy is a(n) ___.

Understanding Key Ideas

5. Which of the following factors affects the resistance of an object?
   a. thickness of the object
   b. length of the object
   c. temperature of the object
   d. All of the above

6. Name the parts of a cell, and explain how they work together to produce an electric current.

7. Compare alternating current with direct current.

8. How do the currents produced by a 1.5 V flashlight cell and a 12 V car battery compare if the resistance is the same?

9. How does increasing the resistance affect the current?

Critical Thinking

10. **Making Comparisons** A friend is having trouble studying the types of cells in this section. Explain to your friend how the terms *photocell* and *thermocouple* hold clues that can help him or her remember the type of energy taken in by each device.

11. **Making Inferences** Why do you think some calculators that contain photocells also contain batteries?

12. **Applying Concepts** Which wire would have the lowest resistance: a long, thin iron wire at a high temperature or a short, thick copper wire at a low temperature?

Interpreting Graphics

13. The wires shown below are made of copper and have the same temperature. Which wire should have the lower resistance? Explain your answer.

A   B

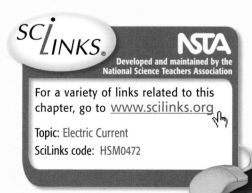

For a variety of links related to this chapter, go to www.scilinks.org

Topic: Electric Current
SciLinks code: HSM0472

Electrical Calculations

A German school teacher named Georg Ohm wondered how electric current, voltage, and resistance are related.

Connecting Current, Voltage, and Resistance

Ohm (1789–1854) studied the resistances of materials. He measured the current that resulted from different voltages applied to a piece of metal wire. The graph on the left in **Figure 1** is similar to the graph of his results.

Ohm's Law

Ohm found that the ratio of voltage (*V*) to current (*I*) is a constant for each material. This ratio is the resistance (*R*) of the material. When the voltage is expressed in volts (V) and the current is in amperes (A), the resistance is in ohms (Ω). The equation below is often called *Ohm's law* because of Ohm's work.

$$R = \frac{V}{I}, \text{ or } V = I \times R$$

As the resistance goes up, the current goes down. And as the resistance decreases, the current increases. The second graph in **Figure 1** shows this relationship. Notice that if you multiply the current and the resistance for any point, you get 16 V.

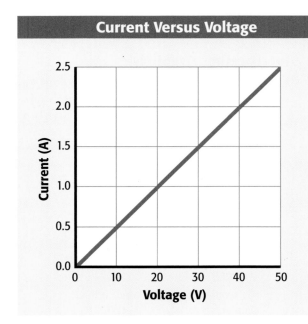

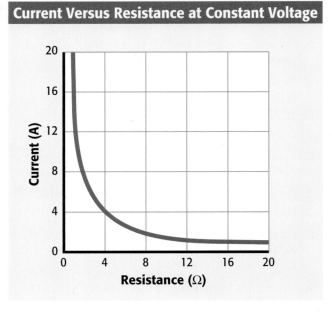

Figure 1 *The relationship between current and voltage is different from the relationship between current and resistance.*

Using Ohm's Law What is the voltage if the current is 2 A and the resistance is 12 Ω?

Step 1: Write the equation for voltage.

$$V = I \times R$$

Step 2: Replace the current and resistance with the measurements given in the problem, and solve.

$$V = 2 \text{ A} \times 12 \text{ Ω}$$
$$V = 24 \text{ V}$$

Now It's Your Turn

1. Find the voltage if the current is 0.2 A and the resistance is 2 Ω.
2. The resistance of an object is 4 Ω. If the current in the object is 9 A, what voltage must be used?
3. An object has a resistance of 20 Ω. Calculate the voltage needed to produce a current of 0.5 A.

Electric Power

The rate at which electrical energy is changed into other forms of energy is **electric power.** The unit for power is the watt (W), and the symbol for power is the letter P. Electric power is expressed in watts when the voltage is in volts and the current is in amperes. Electric power is calculated by using the following equation:

$$\textit{power} = \textit{voltage} \times \textit{current, or } P = V \times I$$

electric power the rate at which electrical energy is converted into other forms of energy

Watt: The Unit of Power

If you have ever changed a light bulb, you probably know about watts. Light bulbs, such as the ones in **Figure 2,** have labels such as "60 W," "75 W," or "120 W." As electrical energy is supplied to a light bulb, the light bulb glows. As power increases, the bulb burns brighter because more electrical energy is converted into light energy. The higher power rating of a 120 W bulb tells you that it burns brighter than a 60 W bulb.

Another common unit of power is the kilowatt (kW). One kilowatt is equal to 1,000 W. Kilowatts are used to express high values of power, such as the power needed to heat a house.

✓ Reading Check What are two common units for electric power? (*See the Appendix for answers to Reading Checks.*)

Figure 2 *These light bulbs have different wattages, so they use different amounts of electric power.*

Measuring Electrical Energy

Electric power companies sell electrical energy to homes and businesses. Such companies determine how much a home or business has to pay based on power and time. For example, the amount of electrical energy used in a home depends on the power of the electrical devices in the house and the length of time that those devices are on. The equation for electrical energy is as follows:

electrical energy = power × time, or $E = P \times t$

Measuring Household Energy Use

Different amounts of electrical energy are used each day in a home. Electric companies usually calculate electrical energy by multiplying the power in kilowatts by the time in hours. The unit of electrical energy is usually kilowatt-hours (kWh). If 2,000 W (2 kW) of power are used for 3 h, then 6 kWh of energy were used.

Electric power companies use meters, such as the one in **Figure 3,** to determine how many kilowatt-hours of energy are used by a household. These meters are often outside of buildings so that someone from the power company can read them.

Reading Check What unit of measurement is usually used to express electrical energy?

Figure 3 *These photographs were taken 10 days apart. According to the dials on the meter, 101 kWh of energy were used.*

MATH FOCUS

Power and Energy A small television set draws a current of 0.42 A at 120 V. What is the power rating for the television? How much energy is used if the television is on for 3 h?

Step 1: Write the equation for power.

$$P = V \times I$$

Step 2: Replace the voltage and current with the measurements given in the problem, and solve.

$$P = 120 \text{ V} \times 0.42 \text{ A}$$
$$P = 50.4 \text{ W, or } 0.0504 \text{ kW}$$

Step 3: Write the equation for electrical energy.

$$E = P \times t$$

Step 4: Replace the power and time with the measurements given in the problem, and solve.

$$E = 0.0504 \text{ kW} \times 3 \text{ h}$$
$$E = 0.1512 \text{ kWh}$$

Now It's Your Turn

1. A computer monitor draws 1.2 A at a voltage of 120 V. What is the power rating of the monitor?
2. A light bulb draws a 0.5 A current at a voltage of 120 V. What is the power rating of the light bulb?
3. How much electrical energy does a 100 W light bulb use if it is left on for 24 h?

How to Save Energy

Every appliance uses energy. But a fan, such as the one in **Figure 4,** could actually help you save energy. If you use a fan, you can run an air conditioner less. Replacing items that have high power ratings with items that have lower ratings is another way to save energy. Turning off lights when they are not in use will also help.

Figure 4 *Using a fan to stay cool and using a small toaster instead of a larger toaster oven are ways to save energy.*

SECTION Review

Summary

- Ohm's law describes the relationship between current, resistance, and voltage.
- Electric power is the rate at which electrical energy is changed into other forms of energy.
- Electrical energy is electric power multiplied by time. It is usually expressed in kilowatt-hours.

Using Key Terms

1. In your own words, write a definition for the term *electric power*.

Understanding Key Ideas

2. Which of the following is Ohm's law?
   a. $E = P \times t$
   b. $I = V \times R$
   c. $P = V \times I$
   d. $V = I \times R$

3. Circuit A has twice the resistance of circuit B. The voltage is the same in each circuit. Which circuit has the higher current?

Math Skills

4. Use Ohm's law to find the voltage needed to make a current of 3 A in a resistance of 9 Ω.

5. How much electrical energy does a 40 W light bulb use if it is left on for 12 h?

Critical Thinking

6. **Applying Concepts** Explain why increasing the voltage applied to a wire can have the same effect on the current in the wire that decreasing the resistance of the wire does.

7. **Identifying Relationships** Using the equations in this section, develop an equation to find electrical energy from time, current, and resistance.

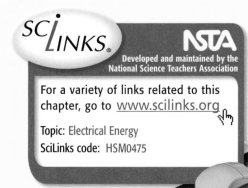

Electric Circuits

Think about a roller coaster. You start out nice and easy. Then, you roar around the track. A couple of exciting minutes later, you are right back where you started!

A roller-coaster car follows a fixed pathway. The ride's starting point and ending point are the same place. This kind of closed pathway is called a *circuit*.

Parts of an Electric Circuit

Just like a roller coaster, an electric circuit always forms a loop—it begins and ends in the same place. Because a circuit forms a loop, a circuit is a closed path. So, an *electric circuit* is a complete, closed path through which electric charges flow.

All circuits need three basic parts: an energy source, wires, and a load. Loads, such as a light bulb or a radio, are connected to the energy source by wires. Loads change electrical energy into other forms of energy. These other forms might include thermal energy, light energy, or mechanical energy. As loads change electrical energy into other forms, they offer some resistance to electric currents. **Figure 1** shows examples of the parts of a circuit.

✓ Reading Check What are the three parts of an electric circuit? (*See the Appendix for answers to Reading Checks.*)

READING WARM-UP

Objectives

● Name the three essential parts of a circuit.

● Compare series circuits with parallel circuits.

● Explain how fuses and circuit breakers protect your home against short circuits and circuit overloads.

Terms to Learn

series circuit
parallel circuit

READING STRATEGY

Brainstorming The key idea of this section is electric circuits. Brainstorm words and phrases related to electric circuits.

Figure 1 **Necessary Parts of a Circuit**

The **energy source** can be a battery, a photocell, a thermocouple, or an electric generator at a power plant.

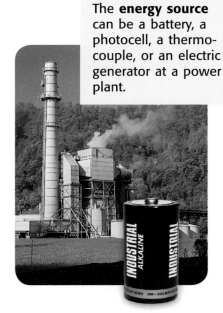

Wires connect the other parts of a circuit. Wires are made of conducting materials that have low resistance, such as copper.

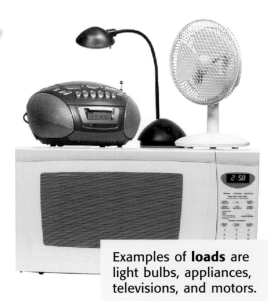

Examples of **loads** are light bulbs, appliances, televisions, and motors.

Figure 2 Using a Switch

When the **switch is closed,** the two pieces of conducting material touch, which allows the electric charges to flow through the circuit.

When the **switch is open,** the gap between the two pieces of conducting material prevents the electric charges from traveling through the circuit.

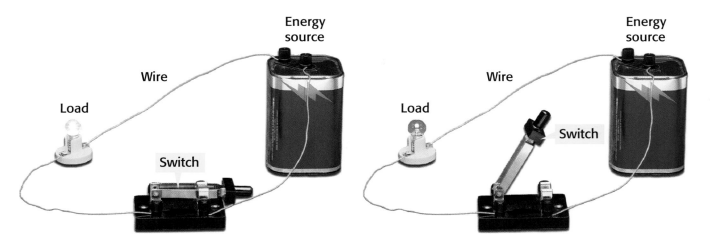

A Switch To Control a Circuit

Sometimes, a circuit also contains a switch, such as the one shown in **Figure 2.** A switch is used to open and close a circuit. Usually, a switch is made of two pieces of conducting material, one of which can be moved. For charges to flow through a circuit, the switch must be closed, or "turned on." If a switch is open, or "off," the loop of the circuit is broken. Charges cannot flow through a broken circuit. Light switches, power buttons on radios, and even the keys on calculators and computers open and close circuits.

Types of Circuits

Look around the room. Count the number of objects that use electrical energy. You might have found things, such as lights, a clock, and maybe a computer. All of the things you counted are loads in a large circuit. The circuit may connect more than one room in the building. In fact, most circuits have more than one load.

The loads in a circuit can be connected in different ways. As a result, circuits are often divided into two types. A circuit can be a series circuit or a parallel circuit. One of the main differences in these circuits is the way in which the loads are connected to one another. As you read about each type of circuit, look closely at how the loads are connected.

CONNECTION TO Biology

WRITING SKILL **Nervous Impulses** Believe it or not, your body is controlled and monitored by electrical impulses. Research the electrical impulses that travel between your brain and the muscles and organs in your body. Then, in your **science journal,** write a one-page comparison of your nervous system and an electric circuit.

Reading Check What are two types of electric circuits?

Series Circuits

A **series circuit** is a circuit in which all parts are connected in a single loop. There is only one path for charges to follow, so the charges moving through a series circuit must flow through each part of the circuit.

All of the loads in a series circuit share the same current. The four identical light bulbs in **Figure 3** are joined in series. Because the current in each bulb is the same, the lights glow with the same brightness. But if you add more light bulbs, the resistance of the whole circuit would go up and the current would drop. Therefore, all of the bulbs would be dimmer.

✓ **Reading Check** How are loads connected in a series circuit?

Uses for Series Circuits

A series circuit has only one pathway for moving charges. If there is any break in the circuit, the charges will stop flowing. For example, if one light bulb in a series circuit burns out, there is a break in the circuit. None of the light bulbs in the circuit would light. Using series circuits would not be a very convenient way to wire your home. Imagine if your refrigerator and a lamp were in a series circuit together. Your refrigerator would run only when the lamp was on. And when the bulb burns out, the refrigerator would stop working!

But series circuits are useful in some ways. For example, series circuits are useful in wiring burglar alarms. If any part of the circuit in a burglar alarm fails, there will be no current in the system. The lack of current signals that a problem exists, and the alarm will sound.

A Series of Circuits

1. Connect a **6 V battery** and **two flashlight bulbs** in a series circuit. Draw a picture of your circuit.

2. Add **another flashlight bulb** in series with the other two bulbs. How does the brightness of the light bulbs change?

3. Replace one of the light bulbs with a **burned-out light bulb.** What happens to the other lights in the circuit? Why?

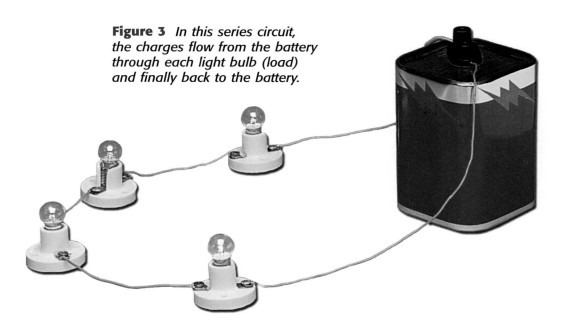

Figure 3 *In this series circuit, the charges flow from the battery through each light bulb (load) and finally back to the battery.*

Parallel Circuits

Think about what would happen if all of the lights in your home were connected in series. If you needed to turn on a light in your room, all other lights in the house would have to be turned on, too! Instead of being wired in series, circuits in buildings are wired in parallel. A **parallel circuit** is a circuit in which loads are connected side by side. Charges in a parallel circuit have more than one path on which they can travel.

Unlike the loads in a series circuit, the loads in a parallel circuit do not have the same current. Instead, each load in a parallel circuit uses the same voltage. For example, each bulb in **Figure 4** uses the full voltage of the battery. As a result, each light bulb glows at full brightness no matter how many bulbs are connected in parallel. You can connect loads that need different currents to the same parallel circuit. For example, you can connect a hair dryer, which needs a high current to run, to the same circuit as a lamp, which needs less current.

Reading Check How are loads connected in a parallel circuit?

Uses for Parallel Circuits

In a parallel circuit, each branch of the circuit can work by itself. If one load is broken or missing, charges will still run through the other branches. So, the loads on those branches will keep working. In your home, each electrical outlet is usually on its own branch and has its own switch. Imagine if each time a light bulb went out your television or stereo stopped working. With parallel circuits, you can use one light or appliance at a time, even if another load fails.

parallel circuit a circuit in which the parts are joined in branches such that the potential difference across each part is the same

A Parallel Lab

1. Connect a **6 V battery** and **two flashlight bulbs** in a parallel circuit. Draw a picture of your circuit.

2. Add **another flashlight bulb** in parallel with the other two bulbs. How does the brightness of the light bulbs change?

3. Replace one of the light bulbs with a **burned-out light bulb.** What happens to the other lights in the circuit? Why?

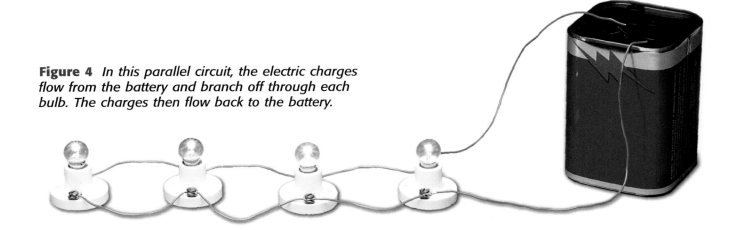

Figure 4 *In this parallel circuit, the electric charges flow from the battery and branch off through each bulb. The charges then flow back to the battery.*

Household Circuit Safety

In every home, several circuits connect all of the lights, appliances, and outlets. The circuits branch out from a breaker box or a fuse box that acts as the "electrical headquarters" for the building. Each branch receives a standard voltage, which is 120 V in the United States.

Circuit Failure

Broken wires or water can cause a short circuit. In a short circuit, charges do not go through one or more loads in the circuit. The resistance decreases, so the current increases. The wires can heat up, and the circuit could fail. The wires might even get hot enough to start a fire. Circuits also may fail if they are overloaded. When too many loads are in a circuit, the current increases, and a fire might start. Safety features, such as fuses and circuit breakers, help prevent electrical fires.

Fuses

A fuse has a thin strip of metal. The charges in the circuit flow through this strip. If the current is too high, the metal strip melts, as shown in **Figure 5.** As a result, the circuit is broken, and charges stop flowing.

Figure 5 *The blown fuse on the left must be replaced with a new fuse, such as the one on the right.*

Circuit Breakers

A circuit breaker is a switch that automatically opens if the current is too high. A strip of metal in the breaker warms up, bends, and opens the switch, which opens the circuit. Charges stop flowing. Open circuit breakers can be closed by flipping a switch after the problem has been fixed.

A ground fault circuit interrupter (GFCI), shown in **Figure 6,** acts as a small circuit breaker. If the current in one side of an outlet differs even slightly from the current in the other side, the GFCI opens the circuit and the charges stop flowing. To close the circuit, you must push the reset button.

Reading Check What are two safety devices used in circuits?

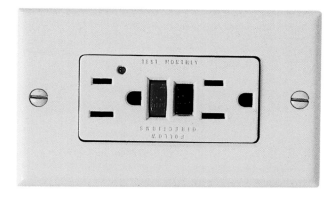

Figure 6 *GFCIs are often found on outlets in bathrooms and kitchens to protect you from electric shock.*

Electrical Safety Tips

You use electrical devices every day. So, remembering that using electrical energy can be hazardous is important. Warning signs, such as the one in **Figure 7,** can help you avoid electrical dangers. To stay safe while you use electrical energy, follow these tips:

- Make sure the insulation on cords is not worn.
- Do not overload circuits by plugging in too many electrical devices.
- Do not use electrical devices while your hands are wet or while you are standing in water.
- Never put objects other than a plug into an electrical outlet.

Figure 7 *Obeying signs that warn of high voltage can keep you safe from electrical dangers.*

SECTION
Review

Summary

- Circuits consist of an energy source, a load, wires, and, in some cases, a switch.
- All parts of a series circuit are connected in a single loop. The loads in a parallel circuit are on separate branches.
- Circuits fail through a short circuit or an overload. Fuses or circuit breakers protect against circuit failure.
- It is important to follow safety tips when using electrical energy.

Using Key Terms

1. In your own words, write a definition for each of the following terms: *series circuit* and *parallel circuit.*

Understanding Key Ideas

2. Which part of a circuit changes electrical energy into another form of energy?
   a. energy source
   b. wire
   c. switch
   d. load

3. Name and describe the three essential parts of a circuit.

4. How do fuses and circuit breakers protect your home against electrical fires?

Critical Thinking

5. **Forming Hypotheses** Suppose that you turn on the heater in your room and all of the lights in your room go out. Propose a reason why the lights went out.

6. **Applying Concepts** Will a fuse work successfully if it is connected in parallel with the device it is supposed to protect? Explain your answer.

Interpreting Graphics

7. Look at the circuits below. Identify each circuit as a parallel circuit or a series circuit.

Ⓐ

Ⓑ

Skills Practice Lab

Circuitry 101

There are two basic types of electric circuits. A series circuit connects all of the parts in a single loop, and a parallel circuit connects each part on a separate branch. A switch wired in series with the energy source can control the whole circuit. If you want each part of the circuit to work on its own, the loads must be wired in parallel. In this lab, you will use an ammeter to measure current and a voltmeter to measure voltage. For each circuit, you will use Ohm's law (resistance equals voltage divided by current) to determine the overall resistance.

Procedure

1 Build a series circuit with an energy source, a switch, and three light bulbs. Draw a diagram of your circuit. **Caution:** Always leave the switch open when building or changing the circuit. Close the switch only when you are testing or taking a reading.

2 Test your circuit. Do all three bulbs light up? Are all bulbs the same brightness? What happens if you carefully unscrew one light bulb? Does it make any difference which bulb you unscrew? Record your observations.

3 Connect the ammeter between the power source and the switch. Close the switch, and record the current on your diagram. Be sure to show where you measured the current.

4 Reconnect the circuit so that the ammeter is between the first and second bulbs. Record the current, as you did in step 3.

5 Move the ammeter so that it is between the second and third bulbs, and record the current again.

6 Remove the ammeter from the circuit. Connect the voltmeter to the two ends of the power source. Record the voltage on your diagram.

7 Use the voltmeter to measure the voltage across each bulb. Record each reading.

8 Take apart your series circuit. Reassemble the same items so that the bulbs are wired in parallel. (Note: The switch must remain in series with the power source to be able to control the whole circuit.) Draw a diagram of your circuit.

OBJECTIVES

Build a series circuit and a parallel circuit.

Use Ohm's law to calculate the resistance of a circuit from voltage and current.

MATERIALS

- ammeter
- energy source—dry cell(s)
- light-bulb holders (3)
- light bulbs (3)
- switch
- voltmeter
- wire, insulated, 15 cm lengths with both ends stripped

SAFETY

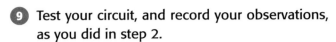

9 Test your circuit, and record your observations, as you did in step 2.

10 Connect the ammeter between the power source and the switch. Record the current.

11 Reconnect the circuit so that the ammeter is right next to one of the three bulbs. Record the current.

12 Repeat step 11 for the two remaining bulbs.

13 Remove the ammeter from your circuit. Connect the voltmeter to the two ends of the power source. Record the voltage.

14 Measure and record the voltage across each light bulb.

Analyze the Results

1 **Recognizing Patterns** Was the current the same at all places in the series circuit? Was it the same everywhere in the parallel circuit?

2 **Analyzing Data** For each circuit, compare the voltage across each light bulb with the voltage at the power source.

3 **Identifying Patterns** What is the relationship between the voltage at the power source and the voltages at the light bulbs in a series circuit?

4 **Analyzing Data** Use Ohm's law and the readings for current (I) and voltage (V) at the power source for both circuits to calculate the total resistance (R) in both the series and parallel circuits.

Draw Conclusions

5 **Drawing Conclusions** Was the total resistance for both circuits the same? Explain your answer.

6 **Interpreting Information** Why did the bulbs differ in brightness?

7 **Making Predictions** Based on your results, what do you think might happen if too many electrical appliances are plugged into the same series circuit? What might happen if too many electrical appliances are plugged into the same parallel circuit?

Chapter Review

USING KEY TERMS

The statements below are false. For each statement, replace the underlined term to make a true statement.

1 Charges flow easily in an <u>electrical insulator</u>.

2 Lightning is a form of <u>static electricity</u>.

3 A <u>thermocouple</u> converts chemical energy into electrical energy.

4 <u>Voltage</u> is the opposition to the current by a material.

5 <u>Electric force</u> is the rate at which electrical energy is converted into other forms of energy.

6 Each load in a <u>parallel circuit</u> has the same current.

UNDERSTANDING KEY IDEAS

Multiple Choice

7 Two objects repel each other. What charges might the objects have?

  a. positive and positive

  b. positive and negative

  c. negative and negative

  d. Both (a) and (c)

8 Which device converts chemical energy into electrical energy?

  a. lightning rod

  b. cell

  c. light bulb

  d. switch

9 Which of the following wires has the lowest resistance?

  a. a short, thick copper wire at 25°C

  b. a long, thick copper wire at 35°C

  c. a long, thin copper wire at 35°C

  d. a short, thick iron wire at 25°C

10 An object becomes charged when the atoms in the object gain or lose

  a. protons.

  b. neutrons.

  c. electrons.

  d. All of the above

11 Which of the following devices does NOT protect you from electrical fires?

  a. electric meter

  b. circuit breaker

  c. fuse

  d. ground fault circuit interrupter

12 For a cell to produce a current, the electrodes of the cell must

  a. have a potential difference.

  b. be in a liquid.

  c. be exposed to light.

  d. be at two different temperatures.

13 The outlets in your home provide

  a. direct current.

  b. alternating current.

  c. electric discharge.

  d. static electricity.

Short Answer

14 Describe how a switch controls a circuit.

15 Name the two factors that affect the strength of electric force, and explain how they affect electric force.

16 Describe how direct current differs from alternating current.

Math Skills

17 What voltage is needed to produce a 6 A current in an object that has a resistance of 3 Ω?

18 Find the current produced when a voltage of 60 V is applied to a resistance of 15 Ω.

19 What is the resistance of an object if a voltage of 40 V produces a current of 5 A?

20 A light bulb is rated at 150 W. How much current is in the bulb if 120 V is applied to the bulb?

21 How much electrical energy does a 60 W light bulb use if it is used for 1,000 hours?

CRITICAL THINKING

22 Concept Mapping Use the following terms to create a concept map: *electric current, battery, charges, photocell, thermocouple, circuit, parallel circuit,* and *series circuit.*

23 Making Inferences Suppose your science classroom was rewired over the weekend. On Monday, you notice that the lights in the room must be on for the fish-tank bubbler to work. And if you want to use the computer, you must turn on the overhead projector. Describe what mistake the electrician made when working on the circuits in your classroom.

24 Applying Concepts You can make a cell by using an apple, a strip of copper, and a strip of silver. Explain how you would construct the cell, and identify the parts of the cell. What type of cell did you make? Explain your answer.

25 Applying Concepts Your friend shows you a magic trick. First, she rubs a plastic pipe on a piece of wool. Then, she holds the pipe close to an empty soda can that is lying on its side. When the pipe is close to the can, the can rolls toward the pipe. Explain how this trick works.

INTERPRETING GRAPHICS

26 Classify the objects in the photograph below as electrical conductors or electrical insulators.

Standardized Test Preparation

Read each of the passages below. Then, answer the questions that follow each passage.

Passage 1 In 1888, Frank J. Sprague developed a way to operate trolleys by using electrical energy. These electric trolleys ran on a metal track and were connected by a pole to an overhead power line. Electric charges flowed down the pole to motors in the trolley. A wheel at the top of the pole, called a <u>shoe</u>, rolled along the power line and allowed the trolley to move along its track without losing contact with its source of electrical energy. The charges passed through the motor and then returned to a generator by way of the metal track.

1. In this passage, what does the word <u>shoe</u> mean?
   - **A** a type of covering that you wear on your foot
   - **B** a device that allowed a trolley to get electrical energy
   - **C** a flat, U-shaped metal plate nailed to a horse's hoof
   - **D** the metal track on which trolleys ran

2. What is the main purpose of this passage?
   - **F** to inform the reader
   - **G** to influence the reader's opinion
   - **H** to express the author's opinion
   - **I** to make the reader laugh

3. Which of the following statements describes what happens first in the operation of a trolley?
   - **A** Charges flow down the pole.
   - **B** Charges pass through the motor.
   - **C** Charges enter the shoe from the power line.
   - **D** Charges return to the generator through the tracks.

Passage 2 Benjamin Franklin (1706–1790) first suggested the terms *positive* and *negative* for the two types of charge. At the age of 40, Franklin was a successful printer and journalist. He saw some experiments on electricity and was so fascinated by them that he began to devote much of his time to experimenting. Franklin was the first person to realize that lightning is a huge electric discharge, or spark. He invented the first lightning rod, for which he became famous. He also flew a kite into thunderclouds—at great risk to his life—to collect charge from them. During and after the Revolutionary War, Franklin gained fame as a politician and a statesman.

1. Which of the following happened earliest in Franklin's life?
   - **A** He gained fame as a politician.
   - **B** He flew a kite into thunderclouds.
   - **C** He saw experiments on electricity.
   - **D** He was a successful journalist.

2. Which of the following statements is a fact according to the passage?
   - **F** Franklin became interested in electricity in 1706.
   - **G** There is no connection between lightning and an electric discharge.
   - **H** Franklin became a successful journalist after he performed experiments with electricity.
   - **I** Flying a kite into thunderclouds is dangerous.

Use the diagram below to answer the questions that follow.

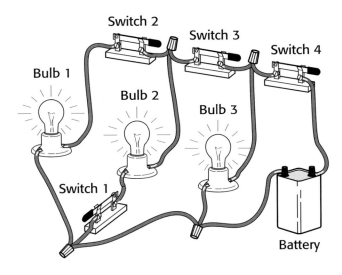

1. Opening which switch will turn off only light bulb 2?

   A switch 1

   B switch 2

   C switch 3

   D switch 4

2. Opening which switch will turn off exactly two light bulbs?

   F switch 1

   G switch 2

   H switch 3

   I switch 4

3. If only switches 2 and 3 are open, which of the following will happen?

   A All three bulbs will remain lit.

   B Only bulb 1 will remain lit.

   C Only bulb 3 will remain lit.

   D All three bulbs will turn off.

4. Which of the following statements is false?

   F Bulb 2 will be off when bulb 1 is off.

   G Bulb 3 will be on if any other bulb is on.

   H Bulbs 1 and 3 can be on when bulb 2 is off.

   I Bulb 3 can be on when bulbs 1 and 2 are off.

Read each question below, and choose the best answer.

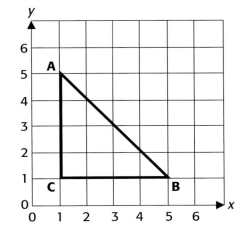

1. Look at triangle *ABC*. If you want to draw square *ADBC*, what would the coordinates of *D* be?

   A (1, 5)

   B (3, 3)

   C (5, 5)

   D (5, 1)

2. The equation *voltage = current × resistance* is often called *Ohm's law*. If the current in an object is 0.5 A and the voltage across the object is 12 V, what is the resistance of the object?

   F 0.042 Ω

   G 6 Ω

   H 12.5 Ω

   I 24 Ω

3. Heather has six large dogs. In one day, each of the dogs eats 2.1 kg of dog food. Which is the best estimate of the total number of kilograms of food all of the dogs eat in 4 weeks?

   A less than 150 kg

   B between 150 and 225 kg

   C between 225 and 300 kg

   D more than 300 kg

Standardized Test Preparation

Science in Action

Weird Science

Electric Eels

Electric eels are freshwater fish from Central and South America. They can produce powerful jolts of electrical energy. Electric discharges from eels are strong enough to stun or kill smaller fish and frogs in the water. The eels then swallow their motionless prey whole. Early travelers to the Amazon River basin wrote that in shallow pools, the eels' discharges could knock horses and humans over. Within the body of an eel, which is 2.5 m long, are a series of electroplates, or modified muscle tissues that generate low voltages. An eel has 5,000 to 6,000 connected electroplates. In lab experiments, the bursts of voltage from a fully grown eel have been measured to be about 600 V.

Math ACTiViTY

The battery in a car provides 12 V. How many times more voltage can a fully grown eel provide than can a car battery? If the voltage provided by the eel were used in a circuit that had a resistance of 200 Ω, what would the current in the circuit be?

Scientific Discoveries

Sprites and Elves

Imagine that you are in a plane on a moonless night. You notice a thunderstorm 80 km away and see lightning move between the clouds and the Earth. Then, suddenly, a ghostly red glow stretches many kilometers above the clouds! You did not expect that!

In 1989, scientists captured the first image of this strange, red, glowing lightning. Since then, photographs from space shuttles, airplanes, telescopes, and observers on the ground have shown several types of electrical glows. Two were named sprites and elves because, like the mythical creatures, they disappear just as the eye begins to see them. Sprites and elves last only a few thousandths of a second.

Language Arts ACTiViTY

WRITING SKILL Imagine that you are a hunter living in about 5000 BCE. On a hunt, you see a sprite as described above. Write a two-page short story explaining what you saw, what your reaction was, and why you think the sprite happened.

Pete Perez

Electrician Sometimes, you forget just how much of daily life is dependent on electricity—until the electricity goes out! Then, you call an electrician, such as Pete Perez. Perez has been installing electrical systems and solving electricity problems in commercial and residential settings since 1971. "I'm in this work because of the challenge. Everywhere you go it's something new."

An electrician performs a wide variety of jobs that may include repairs, routine maintenance, or disaster prevention. One day, he or she might install wiring in a new house. The next day, he or she might replace wiring in an older house. Jobs can be as simple as replacing a fuse or as complicated as restoring an industrial machine. Also, electricians may work under many different conditions, including in a dark basement or at the top of an electrical tower. Perez's advice to aspiring young electricians is, "Open up your mind." You never know what kind of job is waiting for you around the corner, because every day brings stranger and more interesting challenges.

Social Studies ACTIVITY

Imagine that you are helping run a job fair at your school. Research the requirements for becoming an electrician. Make a brochure that tells what an electrician does and what training is needed. Describe how much the training and basic equipment to get started will cost. Include the starting salary and information about any testing or certification that is needed.

To learn more about these Science in Action topics, visit go.hrw.com and type in the keyword **HP5ELEF.**

Current Science

Check out Current Science® articles related to this chapter by visiting go.hrw.com. Just type in the keyword HP5CS17.

2

Electromagnetism

SECTION **1** **Magnets and Magnetism** **40**

SECTION **2** **Magnetism from Electricity** **48**

SECTION **3** **Electricity from Magnetism** **54**

Chapter Lab **60**

Chapter Review **62**

Standardized Test Preparation **64**

Science in Action **66**

About the PHOTO

Superhot particles at millions of degrees Celsius shoot out of the sun. But they do not escape. They loop back and crash into the sun's surface at more than 100 km/s (223,000 mi/h). The image of Earth has been added to show how large these loops can be. What directs the particles? The particles follow the path of the magnetic field lines of the sun. You depend on magnetic fields in electric motors and generators. And you can use them to show off a good report card on the refrigerator.

PRE-READING ACTIVITY

Graphic Organizer

Comparison Table Before you read the chapter, create the graphic organizer entitled "Comparison Table" described in the **Study Skills** section of the Appendix. Label the columns with "Motor" and "Generator." Label the rows with "Energy in" and "Energy out." As you read the chapter, fill in the table with details about the energy conversion that happens in each device.

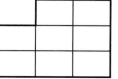

START-UP ACTIVITY

Magnetic Attraction

In this activity, you will investigate ways you can use a magnet to lift steel.

Procedure

1. Put **5 steel paper clips** on your desk. Touch the clips with an **unmagnetized iron nail.** Record the number of clips that stick to it.

2. Touch the clips with the end of a **strong bar magnet.** Record the number of clips that stick to the magnet.

3. While holding the magnet against the head of the nail, touch the tip of the nail to the paper clips. Count the number of paper clips that stick to the nail.

4. Remove the magnet from the end of the nail. Record the number of paper clips you counted in step 3 and your observations when you removed the magnet.

5. Drag one end of the bar magnet 50 times down the nail. Drag the magnet in only one direction.

6. Set the magnet aside. Touch the nail to the clips. Record the number of clips that stick to it.

Analysis

1. What caused the difference between the number of paper clips that you picked up in step 1 and in step 3?

2. What effect did the magnet have on the nail in step 5?

Magnets and Magnetism

You've probably seen magnets stuck to a refrigerator door. These magnets might be holding notes or pictures. Or they might be just for looks.

If you have ever experimented with magnets, you know that they stick to each other and to some kinds of metals. You also know that magnets can stick to things without directly touching them—such as a magnet used to hold a piece of paper to a refrigerator door.

Properties of Magnets

More than 2,000 years ago, the Greeks discovered a mineral that attracted things made of iron. Because this mineral was found in a part of Turkey called Magnesia, the Greeks called it magnetite. Today, any material that attracts iron or things made of iron is called a **magnet.** All magnets have certain properties. For example, all magnets have two poles. Magnets exert forces on each other and are surrounded by a magnetic field.

✓ **Reading Check** What is a magnet? (*See the Appendix for answers to Reading Checks.*)

Magnetic Poles

The magnetic effects are not the same throughout a magnet. What would happen if you dipped a bar magnet into a box of paper clips? Most of the clips would stick to the ends of the bar, as shown in **Figure 1.** This shows that the strongest effects are near the ends of the bar magnet. Each end of the magnet is a magnetic pole. As you will see, **magnetic poles** are points on a magnet that have opposite magnetic qualities.

magnet any material that attracts iron or materials containing iron

magnetic pole one of two points, such as the ends of a magnet, that have opposing magnetic qualities

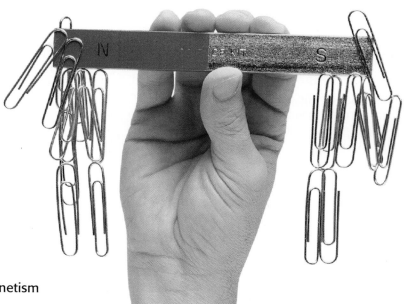

Figure 1 *More paper clips stick to the ends, or magnetic poles, of a magnet because the magnetic effects are strongest there.*

North and South

Suppose you hang a magnet by a string so that the magnet can spin. You will see that one end of the magnet always ends up pointing to the north, as shown in **Figure 2.** The pole of a magnet that points to the north is called the magnet's *north pole*. The opposite end of the magnet points to the south. It is called the magnet's *south pole*. Magnetic poles are always in pairs. You will never find a magnet that has only a north pole or only a south pole.

Magnetic Forces

When you bring two magnets close together, the magnets each exert a **magnetic force** on the other. These magnetic forces result from spinning electric charges in the magnets. The force can either push the magnets apart or pull them together. The magnetic force is a universal force. It is always present when magnetic poles come near one another.

Think of the last time you worked with magnets. If you held two magnets in a certain way, they pulled together. When you turned one of the magnets around, they pushed apart. Why? The magnetic force between magnets depends on how the poles of the magnets line up. Like poles repel, and opposite poles attract, as shown in **Figure 3.**

✔ **Reading Check** If two magnets push each other away, what can you conclude about their poles?

Figure 2 *The needle in a compass is a magnet that is free to rotate.*

magnetic force the force of attraction or repulsion generated by moving or spinning electric charges

---

Figure 3 **Magnetic Force Between Magnets**

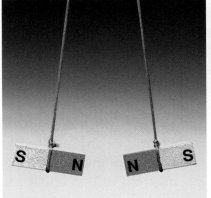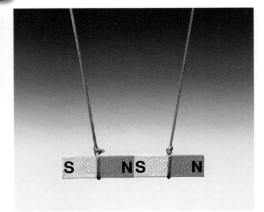

▲ If you hold the north poles of two magnets close together, the magnetic force will push the magnets apart. The same is true if you hold the south poles close together.

▲ If you hold the north pole of one magnet close to the south pole of another magnet, the magnetic force will pull the magnets together.

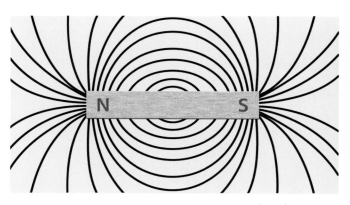 

Figure 4 *Magnetic field lines show the shape of a magnetic field around a magnet. You can model magnetic field lines by sprinkling iron filings around a magnet.*

Magnetic Fields

A *magnetic field* exists in the region around a magnet in which magnetic forces can act. The shape of a magnetic field can be shown with lines drawn from the north pole of a magnet to the south pole, as shown in **Figure 4.** These lines map the strength of the magnetic force and are called *magnetic field lines.* The closer together the field lines are, the stronger the magnetic field is. The lines around a magnet are closest together at the poles, where the magnetic force is strongest.

The Cause of Magnetism

Some materials are magnetic. Some are not. For example, a magnet can pick up paper clips and iron nails. But it cannot pick up paper, plastic, pennies, or aluminum foil. What causes the difference? Whether a material is magnetic depends on the material's atoms.

Atoms and Domains

All matter is made of atoms. Electrons are negatively charged particles of atoms. As an electron moves around, it makes, or induces, a magnetic field. The atom will then have a north and a south pole. In most materials, such as copper and aluminum, the magnetic fields of the individual atoms cancel each other out. Therefore, these materials are not magnetic.

But in materials such as iron, nickel, and cobalt, groups of atoms are in tiny areas called *domains*. The north and south poles of the atoms in a domain line up and make a strong magnetic field. Domains are like tiny magnets of different sizes within an object. The arrangement of domains in an object determines whether the object is magnetic. **Figure 5** shows how the arrangement of domains works.

✓ *Reading Check* **Why are copper and aluminum not magnetic?**

CONNECTION TO Biology

WRITING SKILL **Animal Compasses**
Scientists think that birds and other animals may use Earth's magnetic field to help them navigate. Write a one-page paper in your **science journal** that tells which animals might find their way using Earth's magnetic field. Include evidence scientists have found that supports the idea.

Figure 5 **Arrangement of Domains in an Object**

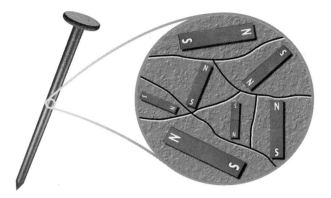

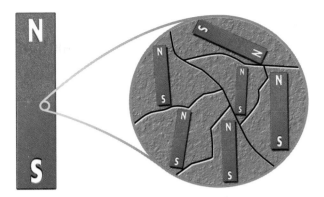

If the domains in an object are randomly arranged, the magnetic fields of the individual domains cancel each other out, and the object has no magnetic properties.

If most of the domains in an object are aligned, the magnetic fields of the individual domains combine to make the whole object magnetic.

Losing Alignment

The domains of a magnet may not always stay lined up. When domains move, the magnet is demagnetized, or loses its magnetic properties. Dropping a magnet or hitting it too hard can move the domains. Putting the magnet in a strong magnetic field that is opposite to its own can also move domains. Increasing the temperature of a magnet can also demagnetize it. At higher temperatures, atoms in the magnet vibrate faster. As a result, the atoms in the domains may no longer line up.

✔️ **Reading Check** Describe two ways a magnet can lose its magnetic properties.

Making Magnets

You can make a magnet from something made of iron, cobalt, or nickel. You just need to line up the domains in it. For example, you can magnetize an iron nail if you rub it in one direction with one pole of a magnet. The domains in the nail line up with the magnetic field of the magnet. So, the domains in the nail become aligned. As more domains line up, the magnetic field of the nail grows stronger. The nail will become a magnet, as shown in **Figure 6.**

The process of making a magnet also explains how a magnet can pick up an unmagnetized object, such as a paper clip. When a magnet is close to a paper clip, some domains in the paper clip line up with the field of the magnet. So, the paper clip becomes a temporary magnet. The north pole of the paper clip points toward the south pole of the magnet. The paper clip is attracted to the magnet. When the magnet is removed, the domains of the paper clip become scrambled again.

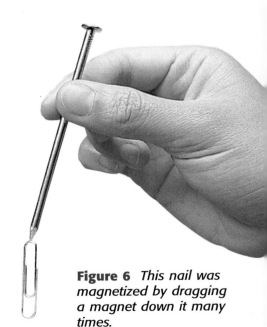

Figure 6 *This nail was magnetized by dragging a magnet down it many times.*

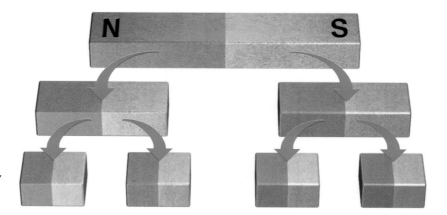

Figure 7 *If you cut a magnet in pieces, each piece will still be a magnet with two poles.*

Cutting a Magnet

What do you think would happen if you cut a magnet in half? You might think that you would end up with one north-pole piece and one south-pole piece. But that's not what happens. When you cut a magnet in half, you end up with two magnets. Each piece has its own north pole and south pole, as shown in **Figure 7.** A magnet has poles because its domains are lined up. Each domain within a magnet is like a tiny magnet with a north pole and a south pole. Even the smallest pieces of a magnet have two poles.

Kinds of Magnets

There are different ways to describe magnets. Some magnets are made of iron, nickel, cobalt, or mixtures of those metals. Magnets made with these metals have strong magnetic properties and are called *ferromagnets*. Look at **Figure 8.** The mineral magnetite is an example of a naturally occurring ferromagnet. Another kind of magnet is the *electromagnet*. This is a magnet made by an electric current. An electromagnet usually has an iron core.

Figure 8 *Magnetite attracts objects containing iron and is a ferromagnet.*

Reading Check What are ferromagnets?

Temporary and Permanent Magnets

Magnets can also be described as temporary magnets or permanent magnets. *Temporary magnets* are made from materials that are easy to magnetize. But they tend to lose their magnetization easily. Soft iron is iron that is not mixed with any other materials. It can be made into temporary magnets. *Permanent magnets* are difficult to magnetize. But they tend to keep their magnetic properties longer than temporary magnets do. Some permanent magnets are made with alnico (AL ni KOH)—an alloy of aluminum, nickel, cobalt, and iron.

Earth as a Magnet

One end of every magnet points to the north if the magnet can spin. For more than 2,000 years, travelers have used this property to find their way. In fact, you use this when you use a compass, because a compass has a freely spinning magnet.

One Giant Magnet

In 1600, an English physician named William Gilbert suggested that magnets point to the north because Earth is one giant magnet. In fact, Earth behaves as if it has a bar magnet running through its center. The poles of this imaginary magnet are located near Earth's geographic poles.

Poles of a Compass Needle

If you put a compass on a bar magnet, the marked end of the needle points to the south pole of the magnet. Does that surprise you? Opposite poles of magnets attract each other. A compass needle is a small magnet. And the tip that points to the north is the needle's north pole. Therefore, the point of a compass needle is attracted to the south pole of a magnet.

South Magnetic Pole near North Geographic Pole

Look at **Figure 9.** A compass needle points north because the magnetic pole of Earth that is closest to the geographic North Pole is a magnetic *south* pole. A compass needle points to the north because its north pole is attracted to a very large magnetic south pole.

Model of Earth's Magnetic Field

1. Place a **bar magnet** on a **sheet of butcher paper.** Draw a circle on the paper with a diameter larger than the bar magnet. This represents the surface of the Earth. Label Earth's North Pole and South Pole.

2. Place the bar magnet under the butcher paper, and line up the bar magnet with the poles.

3. Sprinkle some **iron filings** lightly around the perimeter of the circle. Describe and sketch the pattern you see.

Figure 9 **Earth's Geographic and Magnetic Poles**

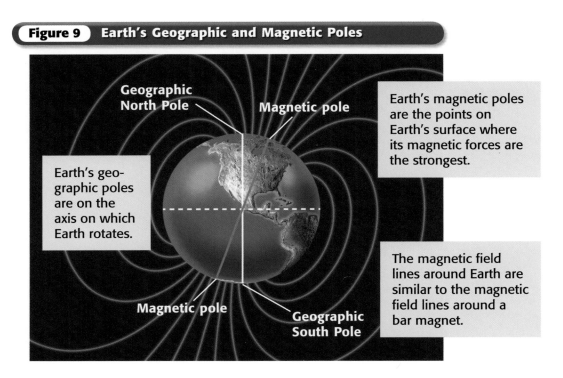

Geographic North Pole

Magnetic pole

Earth's magnetic poles are the points on Earth's surface where its magnetic forces are the strongest.

Earth's geographic poles are on the axis on which Earth rotates.

Magnetic pole

Geographic South Pole

The magnetic field lines around Earth are similar to the magnetic field lines around a bar magnet.

History of the Compass
Records from the first century BCE found in China show that people knew that the mineral lodestone (magnetite) would align to the north. But not until about 1,200 years later were floating compasses used for navigation. Research early compasses, and build a working model of one. Demonstrate to your class how it works.

ACTIVITY

The Core of the Matter

Although you can think of Earth as having a giant bar magnet through its center, there isn't really a magnet there. The temperature of Earth's core (or center) is very high. The atoms in it move too violently to stay lined up in domains.

Scientists think that the Earth's magnetic field is made by the movement of electric charges in the Earth's core. The Earth's core is made mostly of iron and nickel. The inner core is solid because it is under great pressure. The outer core is liquid because the pressure is less. As Earth rotates, the liquid in the core flows. Electric charges move, which makes a magnetic field.

✓ Reading Check What do scientists think causes the Earth's magnetic field?

A Magnetic Light Show

Look at **Figure 10.** The beautiful curtain of light is called an *aurora* (aw RAWR uh). Earth's magnetic field plays a part in making auroras. An aurora is formed when charged particles from the sun hit oxygen and nitrogen atoms in the air. The atoms become excited and then give off light of many colors.

Earth's magnetic field blocks most of the charged particles from the sun. But the field bends inward at the magnetic poles. As a result, the charged particles can crash into the atmosphere at and near the poles. Auroras seen near Earth's North Pole are called the *northern lights,* or aurora borealis (aw RAWR uh BAWR ee AL is). Auroras seen near the South Pole are called the *southern lights,* or aurora australis (aw RAWR uh aw STRAY lis).

Figure 10 *An aurora is an amazing light show in the sky.*

Summary

- All magnets have two poles. The north pole will always point to the north if allowed to rotate freely. The other pole is called the south pole.
- Like magnetic poles repel each other. Opposite magnetic poles attract.
- Every magnet is surrounded by a magnetic field. The shape of the field can be shown with magnetic field lines.
- A material is magnetic if its domains line up.

- Magnets can be classified as ferromagnets, electromagnets, temporary magnets, and permanent magnets.
- Earth acts as if it has a big bar magnet through its core. Compass needles and the north poles of magnets point to Earth's magnetic south pole, which is near Earth's geographic North Pole.
- Auroras are most commonly seen near Earth's magnetic poles because Earth's magnetic field bends inward at the poles.

Using Key Terms

1. Use the following terms in the same sentence: *magnet, magnetic force,* and *magnetic pole.*

Understanding Key Ideas

2. What metal is used to make ferromagnets?
   - **a.** iron
   - **b.** cobalt
   - **c.** nickel
   - **d.** All of the above

3. Name three properties of magnets.

4. Why are some iron objects magnetic and others not magnetic?

5. How are temporary magnets different from permanent magnets?

Critical Thinking

6. **Forming Hypotheses** Why are auroras more commonly seen in places such as Alaska and Australia than in places such as Florida and Mexico?

7. **Applying Concepts** Explain how you could use magnets to make a small object appear to float in air.

8. **Making Inferences** Earth's moon has no atmosphere and has a cool, solid core. Would you expect to see auroras on the moon? Explain your answer.

Interpreting Graphics

The image below shows a model of Earth as a large magnet. Use the image below to answer the questions that follow.

9. Which magnetic pole is closest to the geographic North Pole?

10. Is the magnetic field of Earth stronger near the middle of Earth (in Mexico) or at the bottom of Earth (in Antarctica)? Explain your answer.

Developed and maintained by the National Science Teachers Association

For a variety of links related to this chapter, go to www.scilinks.org

Topic: Magnetism; Types of Magnets
SciLinks code: HSM0900; HSM1566

Magnetism from Electricity

Most of the trains you see roll on wheels on top of a track. But engineers have developed trains that have no wheels. The trains actually float above the track.

READING WARM-UP

Objectives

● Identify the relationship between an electric current and a magnetic field.

● Compare solenoids and electromagnets.

● Describe how electromagnetism is involved in the operation of doorbells, electric motors, and galvanometers.

Terms to Learn

electromagnetism
solenoid
electromagnet
electric motor

READING STRATEGY

Reading Organizer As you read this section, make a table comparing solenoids and electromagnets.

They float because of magnetic forces between the track and the train cars. Such trains are called maglev trains. The name *maglev* is short for magnetic levitation. To levitate, maglev trains use a kind of magnet called an electromagnet. Electromagnets can make strong magnetic fields. In this section, you will learn how electricity and magnetism are related and how electromagnets are made.

The Discovery of Electromagnetism

Danish physicist Hans Christian Oersted (UHR STED) discovered the relationship between electricity and magnetism in 1820. During a lecture, he held a compass near a wire carrying an electric current. Oersted noticed that when the compass was close to the wire, the compass needle no longer pointed to the north. The result surprised Oersted. A compass needle is a magnet. It moves from its north-south orientation only when it is in a magnetic field different from Earth's. Oersted tried a few experiments with the compass and the wire. His results are shown in **Figure 1.**

Figure 1 Oersted's Experiment

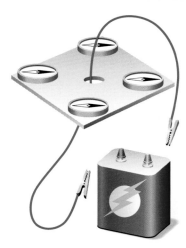 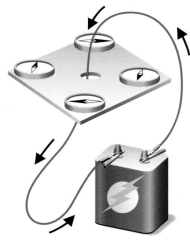 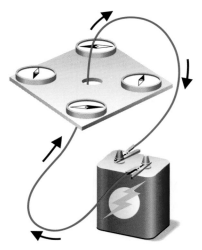

ⓐ If no electric current exists in the wire, the compass needles point in the same direction.

ⓑ Electric current in one direction in the wire causes the compass needles to deflect in a clockwise direction.

ⓒ Electric current in the opposite direction makes the compass needles deflect in a counterclockwise direction.

More Research

From his experiments, Oersted concluded that an electric current produces a magnetic field. He also found that the direction of the field depends on the direction of the current. The French scientist André-Marie Ampère heard about Oersted's findings. Ampère did more research with electricity and magnetism. Their work was the first research of electromagnetism. **Electromagnetism** is the interaction between electricity and magnetism.

✔️ **Reading Check** What is electromagnetism? (*See the Appendix for answers to Reading Checks.*)

electromagnetism the interaction between electricity and magnetism

solenoid a coil of wire with an electric current in it

Using Electromagnetism

The magnetic field generated by an electric current in a wire can move a compass needle. But the magnetic field is not strong enough to be very useful. However, two devices, the solenoid and the electromagnet, strengthen the magnetic field made by a current-carrying wire. Both devices make electromagnetism more useful.

Solenoids

A single loop of wire carrying a current does not have a very strong magnetic field. But suppose you form many loops into a coil. The magnetic fields of the individual loops will combine to make a much stronger field. A **solenoid** is a coil of wire that produces a magnetic field when carrying an electric current. In fact, the magnetic field around a solenoid is very similar to the magnetic field of a bar magnet, as shown in **Figure 2**. The strength of the magnetic field of a solenoid increases as more loops per meter are used. The magnetic field also becomes stronger as the current in the wire is increased.

For another activity related to this chapter, go to **go.hrw.com** and type in the keyword **HP5EMGW**.

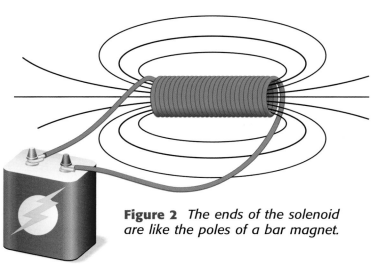

Figure 2 *The ends of the solenoid are like the poles of a bar magnet.*

Quick Lab

Electromagnets

1. Tightly wrap an **insulated copper wire** around a **large iron nail,** and leave 10 cm of wire loose at each end.

2. Use **electrical tape** to attach the bare ends of the wire against the top and bottom of a **D-cell.**

3. Hold the end of the nail near some **paper clips,** and try to lift them up.

4. While holding the clips up, remove the wires from the cell. Then, record your observations.

5. What advantage of electromagnets did you see?

electromagnet a coil that has a soft iron core and that acts as a magnet when an electric current is in the coil

Figure 3 *Electromagnets used in salvage yards are turned on to pick up metal objects and turned off to put them down again.*

Electromagnets

An **electromagnet** is made up of a solenoid wrapped around an iron core. The magnetic field of the solenoid makes the domains inside the iron core line up. The magnetic field of the electromagnet is the field of the solenoid plus the field of the magnetized core. As a result, the magnetic field of an electromagnet may be hundreds of times stronger than the magnetic field of just the solenoid.

You can make an electromagnet even stronger. You can increase the number of loops per meter in the solenoid. You can also increase the electric current in the wire. Some electromagnets are strong enough to lift a car or levitate a train! Maglev trains levitate because strong magnets on the cars are pushed away by powerful electromagnets in the rails.

Reading Check What happens to the magnetic field of an electromagnet if you increase the current in the wire?

Turning Electromagnets On and Off

Electromagnets are very useful because they can be turned on and off as needed. The solenoid has a field only when there is electric current in it. So, electromagnets attract things only when a current exists in the wire. When there is no current in the wire, the electromagnet is turned off. **Figure 3** shows an example of how this property can be useful.

Applications of Electromagnetism

Electromagnetism is useful in your everyday life. You already know that electromagnets can be used to lift heavy objects containing iron. But did you know that you use a solenoid whenever you ring a doorbell? Or that there are electromagnets in motors? Keep reading to learn how electromagnetism makes these things work.

Doorbells

Look at **Figure 4.** Have you ever noticed a doorbell button that has a light inside? Have you noticed that when you push the button, the light goes out? Two solenoids in the doorbell allow the doorbell to work. Pushing the button opens the circuit of the first solenoid. The current stops, causing the magnetic field to drop and the light to go out. The change in the field causes a current in the second solenoid. This current induces a magnetic field that pushes an iron rod that sounds the bell.

Magnetic Force and Electric Current

An electric current can cause a compass needle to move. The needle is a small magnet. The needle moves because the electric current in a wire creates a magnetic field that exerts a force on the needle. If a current-carrying wire causes a magnet to move, can a magnet cause a current-carrying wire to move? **Figure 5** shows that the answer is yes. This property is useful in electric motors.

✓ Reading Check Why does a current-carrying wire cause a compass needle to move?

Figure 4 *Ringing this doorbell requires two solenoids.*

Figure 5 **Magnetic Force on a Current-Carrying Wire**

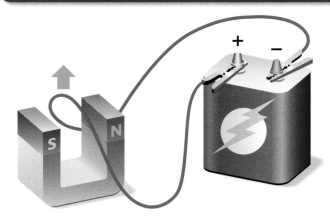

ⓐ When a current-carrying wire is placed between two poles of a magnet, the wire will jump up.

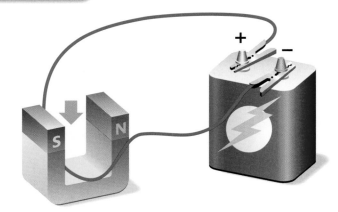

ⓑ Switching the wires at the battery reverses the direction of the current, and the wire is pushed down.

Electric Motors

electric motor a device that converts electrical energy into mechanical energy

An **electric motor** is a device that changes electrical energy into mechanical energy. All electric motors have an *armature*—a loop or coil of wire that can rotate. The armature is mounted between the poles of a permanent magnet or electromagnet.

In electric motors that use direct current, a device called a *commutator* is attached to the armature to reverse the direction of the electric current in the wire. A commutator is a ring that is split in half and connected to the ends of the armature. Electric current enters the armature through brushes that touch the commutator. Every time the armature and the commutator make a half turn, the direction of the current in the armature is reversed. **Figure 6** shows how a direct-current motor works.

Figure 6 A Direct-Current Electric Motor

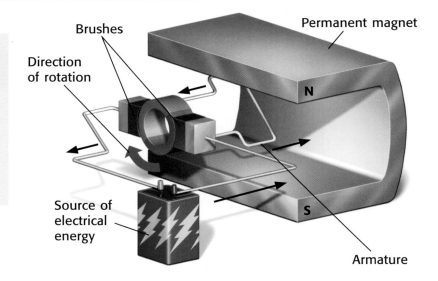

Getting Started An electric current in the armature causes the magnet to exert a force on the armature. Because of the direction of the current on either side of the armature, the magnet pulls up on one side and down on the other side. This pulling makes the armature rotate.

Brushes

Direction of rotation

Permanent magnet

N

Source of electrical energy

S

Armature

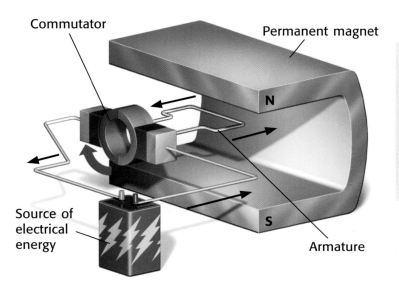

Commutator

Permanent magnet

N

Source of electrical energy

S

Armature

Running the Motor As the armature rotates, the commutator causes the electric current in the coil to change directions. When the electric current is reversed, the side of the coil that was pulled up is pulled down and the side that was pulled down is pulled up. This change of direction keeps the armature rotating.

Galvanometers

A galvanometer (GAL vuh NAHM uht uhr) measures current. Galvanometers are sometimes found in equipment used by electricians, such as ammeters and voltmeters, as shown in **Figure 7.** A galvanometer has an electromagnet placed between the poles of a permanent magnet. The poles of the electromagnet are pushed away by the poles of the permanent magnet. The electromagnet is free to rotate and is attached to a pointer. The pointer moves along a scale that shows the size and direction of the current.

Figure 7 *This ammeter uses a galvanometer to measure electric current.*

✔️ **Reading Check** What does a galvanometer measure?

SECTION Review

Summary

- Oersted discovered that a wire carrying a current makes a magnetic field.
- Electromagnetism is the interaction between electricity and magnetism.
- An electromagnet is a solenoid that has an iron core.
- A magnet can exert a force on a wire carrying a current.
- A doorbell, an electric motor, and a galvanometer all make use of electromagnetism.

Using Key Terms

For each pair of terms, explain how the meanings of the terms differ.

1. *electromagnet* and *solenoid*

Understanding Key Ideas

2. Which of the following actions will decrease the strength of the magnetic field of an electromagnet?
   a. using fewer loops of wire per meter in the coil
   b. decreasing the current in the wire
   c. removing the iron core
   d. All of the above

3. Describe what happens when you hold a compass close to a wire carrying a current.

4. What is the relationship between an electric current and a magnetic field?

5. What makes the armature in an electric motor rotate?

Critical Thinking

6. **Applying Concepts** What do Hans Christian Oersted's experiments have to do with a galvanometer? Explain your answer.

7. **Making Comparisons** Compare the structures and magnetic fields of solenoids with those of electromagnets.

Interpreting Graphics

8. Look at the image below. Your friend says that the image shows an electromagnet because there are loops with a core in the middle. Is your friend correct? Explain your reasoning.

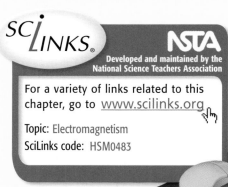

SCLINKS®

NSTA
Developed and maintained by the National Science Teachers Association

For a variety of links related to this chapter, go to www.scilinks.org

Topic: Electromagnetism
SciLinks code: HSM0483

Electricity from Magnetism

When you use an electrical appliance or turn on a light in your home, you probably don't think about where the electrical energy comes from.

For most people, an electric power company supplies their home with electrical energy. In this section, you'll learn how a magnetic field can induce an electric current and how power companies use this process to supply electrical energy.

Electric Current from a Changing Magnetic Field

Hans Christian Oersted discovered that an electric current could make a magnetic field. Soon after, scientists wondered if a magnetic field could make an electric current. In 1831, two scientists each solved this problem. Joseph Henry, of the United States, made the discovery first. But Michael Faraday, from Great Britain, published his results first. Faraday also reported them in great detail, so his results are better known.

Faraday's Experiment

Faraday used a setup like the one shown in **Figure 1.** Faraday hoped that the magnetic field of the electromagnet would make—or induce—an electric current in the second wire. But no matter how strong the electromagnet was, he could not make an electric current in the second wire.

✓ *Reading Check* **What was Faraday trying to do in his experiment?** (*See the Appendix for answers to Reading Checks.*)

Figure 1 **Faraday's Experiment with Magnets and Induction**

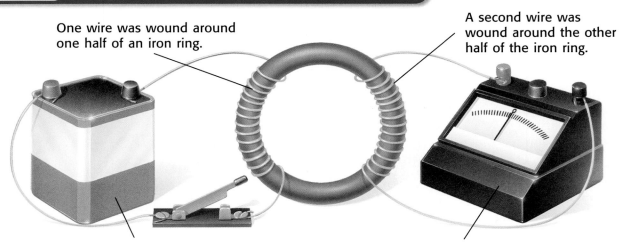

One wire was wound around one half of an iron ring.

A second wire was wound around the other half of the iron ring.

A battery supplied an electric current to the wire, making an electromagnet.

A galvanometer measured any current produced in the second wire by the magnetic field.

Figure 2 Factors that Affect an Induced Current

a An electric current is induced when you move a magnet through a coil of wire.

b A greater electric current is induced if you move the magnet faster through the coil because the magnetic field is changing faster.

c A greater electric current is induced if you add more loops of wire. This magnet is moving at the same speed as the magnet in **b.**

d The induced electric current reverses direction if the magnet is pulled out rather than pushed in.

Success for an Instant

As Faraday experimented with the electromagnetic ring, he noticed something interesting. At the instant he connected the wires to the battery, the galvanometer pointer moved. This movement showed that an electric current was present. The pointer moved again at the instant he disconnected the battery. But as long as the battery was fully connected, the galvanometer measured no electric current.

Faraday realized that electric current in the second wire was made only when the magnetic field was changing. The magnetic field changed as the battery was connected and disconnected. The process by which an electric current is made by changing a magnetic field is called **electromagnetic induction.** Faraday did many more experiments in this area. Some of his results are shown in **Figure 2.**

electromagnetic induction the process of creating a current in a circuit by changing a magnetic field

Figure 3 *As the wire moves between the poles of the magnet, it cuts through magnetic field lines, and an electric current is induced.*

electric generator a device that converts mechanical energy into electrical energy

Inducing Electric Current

Faraday's experiments also showed that moving either the magnet or the wire changes the magnetic field around the wire. So, an electric current is made when a magnet moves in a coil of wire or when a wire moves between the poles of a magnet.

Consider the magnetic field lines between the poles of the magnet. An electric current is induced only when a wire crosses the magnetic field lines, as shown in **Figure 3.** An electric current is induced because a magnetic force can cause electric charges to move. But the charges move in a wire only when the wire moves through the magnetic field.

Electric Generators

Electromagnetic induction is very important for the generation of electrical energy. An **electric generator** uses electromagnetic induction to change mechanical energy into electrical energy. **Figure 4** shows the parts of a simple generator. **Figure 5** explains how the generator works.

✓ **Reading Check** What energy change happens in an electric generator?

Figure 4 **Parts of a Simple Generator**

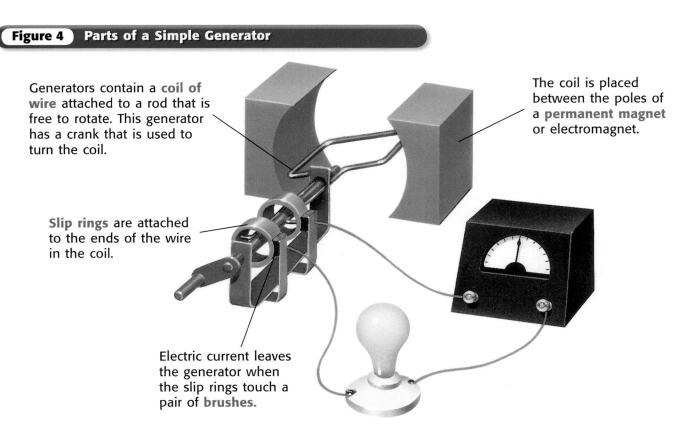

Generators contain a **coil of wire** attached to a rod that is free to rotate. This generator has a crank that is used to turn the coil.

The coil is placed between the poles of a **permanent magnet** or electromagnet.

Slip rings are attached to the ends of the wire in the coil.

Electric current leaves the generator when the slip rings touch a pair of **brushes.**

Figure 5 How a Generator Works

❶ As the crank is turned, the rotating coil crosses the magnetic field lines of the magnet, and an electric current is induced in the wire.

❷ When the coil is not crossing the magnetic field lines, no electric current is induced.

❸ As the coil continues to rotate, the magnetic field lines are crossed in a different direction. An electric current is induced in the opposite direction.

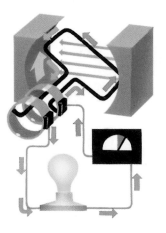

Alternating Current

The electric current produced by the generator shown in **Figure 5** changes direction each time the coil makes a half turn. Because the electric current changes direction, it is an alternating current. Generators in power plants also make alternating current. But generators in power plants are very large. They have many coils of wire instead of just one. In most large generators, the magnet is turned instead of the coils.

Generating Electrical Energy

The energy that generators convert into electrical energy comes from different sources. The source in nuclear power plants is thermal energy from a nuclear reaction. The energy boils water into steam. The steam turns a turbine. The turbine turns the magnet of the generator, which induces an electric current and generates electrical energy. Other kinds of power plants burn fuel such as coal or gas to release thermal energy.

Energy from wind can also be used to turn turbines. **Figure 6** shows how the energy of falling water is converted into electrical energy in a hydroelectric power plant.

✓ Reading Check What are three sources of energy that are used to generate electrical energy?

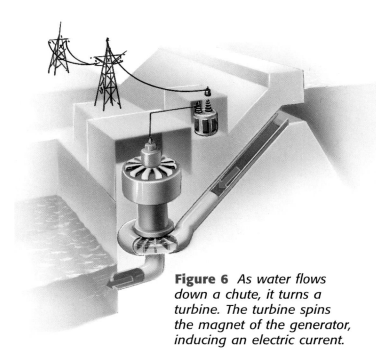

Figure 6 *As water flows down a chute, it turns a turbine. The turbine spins the magnet of the generator, inducing an electric current.*

Figure 7 How Transformers Change Voltage

The primary coil of a **step-up transformer** has fewer loops than the secondary coil. So, the voltage of the electric current in the secondary coil is higher than the voltage of the electric current in the primary coil. Therefore, voltage is increased.

The primary coil of a **step-down transformer** has more loops than the secondary coil. So, the voltage of the electric current in the secondary coil is lower than the voltage of the electric current in the primary coil. Therefore, voltage is decreased.

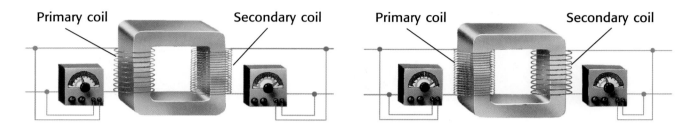

Primary coil   Secondary coil

Primary coil   Secondary coil

transformer a device that increases or decreases the voltage of alternating current

Transformers

Another device that relies on induction is a transformer. A **transformer** increases or decreases the voltage of alternating current. A simple transformer is made up of two coils of wire wrapped around an iron ring. The primary coil gets alternating current from an electrical energy source. The current makes the ring an electromagnet. But the current in the primary coil is alternating. The magnetic field of the electromagnet changes as the direction of the current changes. The changing magnetic field in the iron ring induces a current in the secondary coil.

✓ Reading Check What does a transformer do?

Step-Up, Step-Down

The number of loops in the primary and secondary coils of a transformer determines whether it increases or decreases the voltage, as shown in **Figure 7.** A step-up transformer increases voltage and decreases current. A step-down transformer decreases voltage and increases current. However, the amount of energy going into and out of the transformer does not change.

Electrical Energy for Your Home

The electric current that brings electrical energy to your home is usually transformed three times, as shown in **Figure 8.** At the power plants, the voltage is increased. This decreases power loss that happens as the energy is sent over long distances. Of course, the voltage must be decreased again before the current is used. Two step-down transformers are used before the electric current reaches your house.

Transformers and Voltage

In a transformer, for each coil, the voltage divided by the number of loops must be equal.

What is the voltage in the secondary coil of a transformer that has 20 loops if the primary coil has 10 loops and a voltage of 1,200 V?

Figure 8 Getting Energy to Your Home

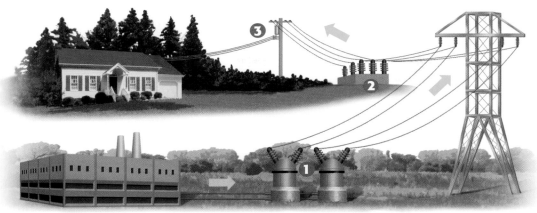

❶ The voltage is stepped up thousands of times at the power plant.

❷ The voltage is stepped down at a local power distribution center.

❸ The voltage is stepped down again at a transformer near your house.

SECTION Review

Summary

- Electromagnetic induction is the process of making an electric current by changing a magnetic field.

- An electric generator converts mechanical energy into electrical energy through electromagnetic induction.

- A step-up transformer increases the voltage of an alternating current. A step-down transformer decreases the voltage.

- The side of a transformer that has the greater number of loops has the higher voltage.

Using Key Terms

For each pair of terms, explain how the meanings of the terms differ.

1. *electric generator* and *transformer*

Understanding Key Ideas

2. Which of the following will induce an electric current in a wire?
   a. moving a magnet into a coil of wire
   b. moving a wire between the poles of a magnet
   c. turning a loop of wire between the poles of a magnet
   d. All of the above

3. How does a generator produce an electric current?

4. Compare a step-up transformer with a step-down transformer based on the number of loops in the primary and secondary coils.

Math Skills

5. A transformer has 500 loops in its primary coil and 5,000 loops in its secondary coil. What is the voltage in the primary coil if the voltage in the secondary coil is 20,000 V?

6. A transformer has 3,000 loops in its primary coil and 1,500 loops in its secondary coil. What is the voltage in the secondary coil if the voltage in the primary coil is 120 V?

Critical Thinking

7. **Analyzing Ideas** One reason that electric power plants do not send out electrical energy as direct current is that direct current cannot be transformed. Explain why not.

8. **Analyzing Processes** Explain why rotating either the coil or the magnet in a generator induces an electric current.

SCI LINKS.

NSTA
Developed and maintained by the National Science Teachers Association

For a variety of links related to this chapter, go to www.scilinks.org

Topic: Electromagnetic Induction
SciLinks code: HSM0481

Model-Making Lab

OBJECTIVES

Build a model of an electric motor.

Analyze the workings of the parts of a motor.

MATERIALS

- battery, 4.5 V
- cup, plastic-foam
- magnet, disc (4)
- magnet wire, 100 cm
- marker, permanent
- paper clips, large (2)
- sandpaper
- tape
- tube, cardboard
- wire, insulated, with alligator clips, approximately 30 cm long (2)

SAFETY

Build a DC Motor

Electric motors can be used for many things. Hair dryers, CD players, and even some cars and buses are powered by electric motors. In this lab, you will build a direct current electric motor—the basis for the electric motors you use every day.

Procedure

1 To make the armature for the motor, wind the wire around the cardboard tube to make a coil like the one shown below. Wind the ends of the wire around the loops on each side of the coil. Leave about 5 cm of wire free on each end.

2 Hold the coil on its edge. Sand the enamel from only the top half of each end of the wire. This acts like a commutator, except that it blocks the electric current instead of reversing it during half of each rotation.

3 Partially unfold the two paper clips from the middle. Make a hook in one end of each paper clip to hold the coil, as shown below.

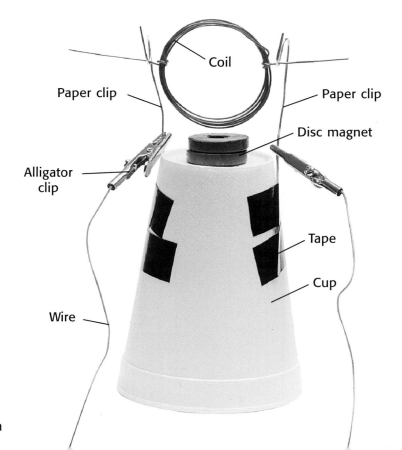

4. Place two disc magnets in the bottom of the cup, and place the other magnets on the outside of the bottom of the cup. The magnets should remain in place when the cup is turned upside down.

5. Tape the paper clips to the sides of the cup. The hooks should be at the same height, and should keep the coil from hitting the magnet.

6. Test your coil. Flick the top of the coil lightly with your finger. The coil should spin freely without wobbling or sliding to one side.

7. Make adjustments to the ends of the wire and the hooks until your coil spins freely.

8. Use the alligator clips to attach one wire to each paper clip.

9. Attach the free end of one wire to one terminal of the battery.

10. Connect the free end of the other wire to the second battery terminal, and give your coil a gentle spin. Record your observations.

11. Stop the coil, and give it a gentle spin in the opposite direction. Record your observations.

12. If the coil does not keep spinning, check the ends of the wire. Bare wire should touch the paper clips during half of the spin, and only enamel should touch the paper clips for the other half of the spin.

13. If you removed too much enamel, color half of the wire with a permanent marker.

14. Switch the connections to the battery, and repeat steps 10 and 11.

Analyze the Results

1. **Describing Events** Did your motor always spin in the direction you started it? Explain.

2. **Explaining Events** Why was the motor affected by switching the battery connections?

3. **Explaining Events** Some electric cars run on solar power. Which part of your model would be replaced by the solar panels?

Draw Conclusions

4. **Drawing Conclusions** Some people claim that electric-powered cars produce less pollution than gasoline-powered cars do. Why might this be true?

5. **Evaluating Models** List some reasons that electric cars are not ideal.

6. **Applying Conclusions** How could your model be used to help design a hair dryer?

7. **Applying Conclusions** Make a list of at least three other items that could be powered by an electric motor like the one you built.

Chapter Review

USING KEY TERMS

Complete each of the following sentences by choosing the correct term from the word bank.

electric motor
magnetic force
magnetic pole
electromagnetic induction

transformer
electric generator
electromagnetism

1 Each end of a bar magnet is a(n) ___.

2 A(n) ___ converts mechanical energy into electrical energy.

3 ___ occurs when an electric current is made by a changing magnetic field.

4 The relationship between electricity and magnetism is called ___.

UNDERSTANDING KEY IDEAS

Multiple Choice

5 The region around a magnet in which magnetic forces can act is called the

a. magnetic field.

b. domain.

c. pole.

d. solenoid.

6 An electric fan has an electric motor inside to change

a. mechanical energy into electrical energy.

b. thermal energy into electrical energy.

c. electrical energy into thermal energy.

d. electrical energy into mechanical energy.

7 The marked end of a compass needle always points directly to

a. Earth's geographic South Pole.

b. Earth's geographic North Pole.

c. a magnet's south pole.

d. a magnet's north pole.

8 A device that increases the voltage of an alternating current is called a(n)

a. electric motor.

b. galvanometer.

c. step-up transformer.

d. step-down transformer.

9 The magnetic field of a solenoid can be increased by

a. adding more loops per meter.

b. increasing the current.

c. putting an iron core inside the coil to make an electromagnet.

d. All of the above

10 What do you end up with if you cut a magnet in half?

a. one north-pole piece and one south-pole piece

b. two unmagnetized pieces

c. two pieces each with a north pole and a south pole

d. two north-pole pieces

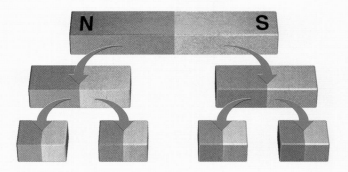

Short Answer

11 Explain why auroras are seen mostly near the North Pole and South Pole.

12 Compare the function of an electric generator with the function of an electric motor.

13 Explain why some pieces of iron are more magnetic than others are.

Math Skills

14 A step-up transformer increases voltage 20 times. If the voltage of the primary coil is 1,200 V, what is the voltage of the secondary coil?

CRITICAL THINKING

15 **Concept Mapping** Use the following terms to create a concept map: *electromagnetism, electricity, magnetism, electromagnetic induction, generators,* and *transformers*.

16 **Applying Concepts** You win a hand-powered flashlight as a prize in your school science fair. The flashlight has a clear plastic case, so you can look inside to see how it works. When you press the handle, a gray ring spins between two coils of wire. The ends of the wire are connected to the light bulb. So, when you press the handle, the light bulb glows. Explain how an electric current is produced to light the bulb. (Hint: Paper clips are attracted to the gray ring.)

17 **Identifying Relationships** Closed fire doors can slow the spread of fire between rooms. In some buildings, electromagnets controlled by the building's fire-alarm system hold the fire doors open. If a fire is detected, the doors automatically shut. Explain why electromagnets are used instead of permanent magnets.

INTERPRETING GRAPHICS

18 Look at the solenoids and electromagnets shown below. Identify which of them has the strongest magnetic field and which has the weakest magnetic field. Explain your reasoning.

a
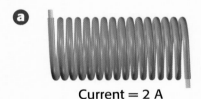
Current = 2 A

b
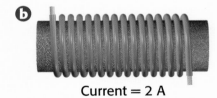
Current = 2 A

c
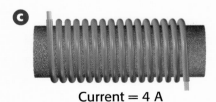
Current = 4 A

d
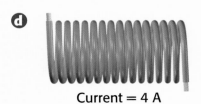
Current = 4 A

READING

Read each of the passages below. Then, answer the questions that follow each passage.

Passage 1 Place a small disk of plastic foam in a bowl of water. Hold the eye of a sewing needle in one hand and a bar magnet in the other. Starting near your fingers, drag one end of the magnet down the needle from the eye to the point and off the end of the needle. Drag the magnet down the needle in the same direction about 20 times. Be sure each stroke uses the same end of the magnet and moves in the same direction down the needle. Carefully place the needle on the plastic foam. The needle and foam should float. Bring the south pole of the magnet near the needle. Note which end of the needle points toward the magnet. Remove the magnet, and observe how the needle turns. The end of the needle that pointed toward the south pole of the magnet will point in a northerly direction.

1. What is the purpose of the passage?
   A to express
   B to instruct
   C to convince
   D to direct

2. What can a person build by following the steps described in the passage?
   F a fishing float
   G a bar magnet
   H an electromagnet
   I a compass

Passage 2 Frogs have been seen floating in midair! No, it's not a magic trick. It's part of an experiment on magnetic levitation. Every object, living or nonliving, contains atoms that act like magnets. These atomic magnets are millions of times weaker than ordinary household magnets. But the atomic magnets are still strong enough to be influenced by other magnets. If an object, such as a frog, is exposed to a magnet that is strong enough, the magnetic force between the object and the magnet can lift the object and make it float. A large solenoid is used in these experiments. A solenoid is a coil of wire that acts like a magnet when an electric current is in the wire. The solenoid has a magnetic field with a north pole and a south pole. The interaction of the magnetic field of the solenoid and the magnetic fields of the atoms in the object causes the object to float.

1. Why can objects be made to float in a magnetic field?
   A Every object has a strong magnetic field.
   B Every object has atoms that have magnetic fields.
   C Every object acts like a solenoid.
   D Every object makes a magnetic field when it is exposed to a household magnet.

2. Which of the following can be inferred from information in the passage?
   F Household magnets cannot levitate in the solenoid used in the experiment.
   G Atomic magnets are stronger than the solenoid used in the experiment.
   H Household magnets are strong enough to levitate a frog.
   I Household magnets are stronger than atomic magnets but weaker than the solenoid used in the experiment.

The graph below shows current versus rotation angle for the output of an alternating-current generator. Use the graph below to answer the questions that follow.

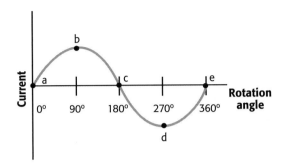

1. Which of the following describes points at which the generator produces no current?

A a and b

B b and d

C c and d

D a and e

2. Between which points is current increasing?

F between a and b

G between b and c

H between c and e

I between b and d

3. At which points is the same amount of current produced but the direction of the current reversed?

A a and b

B b and d

C a and c

D b and e

Read each question below, and choose the best answer.

1. The voltage across the secondary coil of a transformer is found by multiplying the voltage across the primary coil by the number of turns in the secondary coil and then dividing by the number of turns in the primary coil. A certain transformer has a primary coil with 1,000 turns and a voltage of 1,200 V. What is the voltage across the secondary coil if it has 2,000 turns?

A 600 V

B 1,000 V

C 2,400 V

D 2,400,000 V

2. Laura cuts a magnetic strip into thirds. She then cuts each third into halves. How many small magnets does she have?

F 1.5

G 3

H 5

I 6

3. Mrs. Welch is ordering magnets for her science class. She has 24 students in her class, who work in pairs. Each pair of lab partners needs three magnets for the experiment. If Mrs. Welch can order a pack of six magnets for $5.00, what is the cost for her order?

A $2.50

B $30.00

C $60.00

D $120.00

4. A disc magnet is 0.5 cm thick and has a diameter of 2.5 cm. The volume of this magnet in cubic centimeters (cm³) can be calculated using which of the following equations?

F $V = \pi(2.5)^2 \times 0.5$

G $V = \pi(2.5/2)^2 \times 0.5$

H $V = \pi(0.5)^2 \times 2.5$

I $V = \pi(0.5/2)^2 \times 2.5$

Standardized Test Preparation

Science in Action

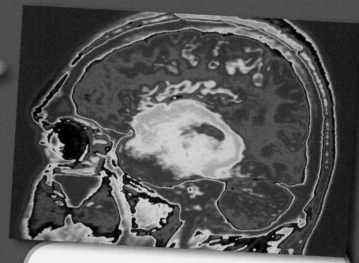

Science, Technology, and Society

Magnets in Medicine

Like X rays, magnetic resonance imaging (MRI) creates pictures of a person's internal organs and skeleton. But MRI produces clearer pictures than X rays do, and MRI does not expose the body to the potentially harmful radiation of X rays. Instead, MRI uses powerful electromagnets and radio waves to create images. MRI allows doctors to find small tumors, see subtle changes in the brain, locate blockages in blood vessels, and observe damage to the spinal cord.

Weird Science

Geomagnetic Storms

On March 13, 1989, a geomagnetic storm hit Montreal, Quebec. It caused an electrical blackout that left about 6 million people without electricity for nine hours.

A geomagnetic storm occurs when gusts of solar wind smash into Earth's magnetic field. Powerful eruptions from the sun, called coronal mass ejections (CME), happen periodically, sending charged particles outward at high speeds. Solar winds usually travel between 300 km/s and 600 km/s. But the gusts of solar wind from a CME can travel as fast as 2,000 km/s.

Language Arts ACTiViTY

WRITING SKILL Write a two-page story about a student who undergoes an MRI scan. In your story, include the reason he or she must have the scan, a description of the procedure, and the information the doctor can determine by looking at the scan.

Math ACTiViTY

Earth is approximately 150,000,000 km from the sun. Calculate how long it takes a solar wind that travels at 500 km/s to reach Earth from the sun.

James Clerk Maxwell

Magnetic Math James Clerk Maxwell was a Scottish mathematician who lived in the 1800s. Maxwell's research led to advances in electromagnetism and in many other areas of science. He proposed that light is an electromagnetic wave—a wave that consists of electric and magnetic fields that vibrate at right angles to each other. His work on electromagnetic fields provided the foundation for Einstein's theory of relativity.

After college, Maxwell decided to study the work of Michael Faraday. Many physicists of the time thought that Faraday's work was not scientific enough. Faraday described his experiments but did not try to apply any scientific or mathematical theory to the results. Maxwell felt that this was a strength. He decided not to read any of the mathematical descriptions of electricity and magnetism until he had read all of Faraday's work. The first paper Maxwell wrote about electricity, called "On Faraday's Lines of Force," brought Faraday's experimental results together with a mathematical analysis of the magnetic field surrounding a current. This paper described a few simple mathematical equations that could be used to describe the interactions between electric and magnetic fields. Maxwell continued to work with Faraday's results and to publish papers that gave scientific explanations of some of Faraday's most exciting observations.

Social Studies ACTiViTY

Study the life of James Clerk Maxwell. Make a timeline that shows major events in his life. Include three or four historic events that happened during his lifetime.

To learn more about these Science in Action topics, visit go.hrw.com and type in the keyword HP5EMGF.

Current Science

Check out Current Science® articles related to this chapter by visiting go.hrw.com. Just type in the keyword HP5CS18.

3

Electronic Technology

SECTION 1 Electronic Devices 70

SECTION 2 Communication Technology 76

SECTION 3 Computers 84

Chapter Lab 92
Chapter Review 94
Standardized Test Preparation 96
Science in Action 98

About the PHOTO

Can you read the expression on Kismet's face? This robot's expression can be sad, happy, angry, interested, surprised, disgusted, or just plain calm. Kismet was developed by MIT researchers to interact with humans. Electronic devices in cameras, motors, and computers allow Kismet to change its expression as it responds to its surroundings.

PRE-READING ACTIVITY

FOLDNOTES **Booklet** Before you read the chapter, create the FoldNote entitled "Booklet" described in the **Study Skills** section of the Appendix. Label each page of the booklet with a main idea from the chapter. As you read the chapter, write what you learn about each main idea on the appropriate page of the booklet.

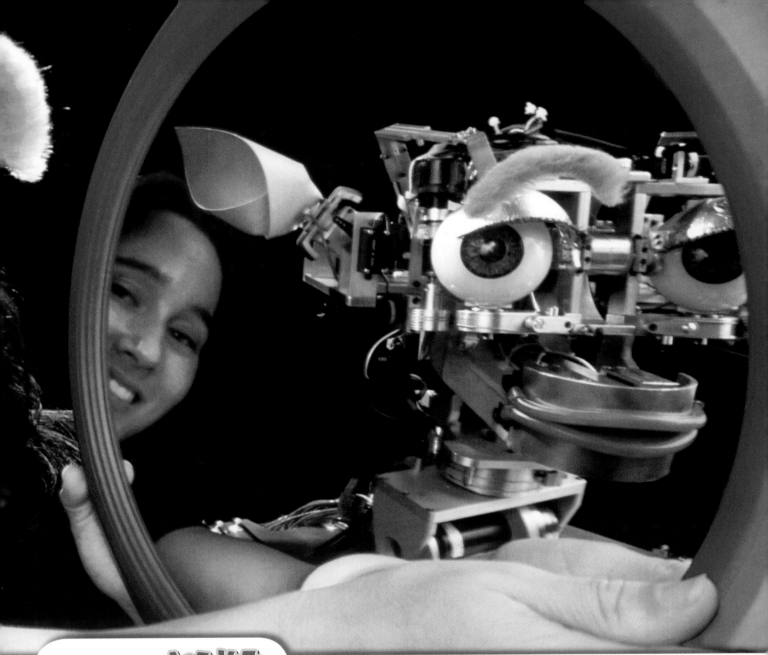

START-UP ACTIVITY

Talking Long Distance

In this activity, you'll build a model of a telephone.

Procedure

1. Thread one end of a **piece of string** through the hole in the bottom of one **empty food can.**

2. Tie a knot in the end of the string inside the can. The knot should be large enough to keep the string in place. The rest of the string should come out of the bottom of the can.

3. Repeat steps 1 and 2 with **another can** and the other end of the string.

4. Hold one can, and have a classmate hold the other. Walk away from each other until the string is fairly taut.

5. Speak into your can while your classmate holds the other can at his or her ear. Switch roles.

Analysis

1. Describe what you heard.

2. Compare your model with a real telephone.

3. How are signals sent back and forth along the string?

4. Why do you think it was important to pull the string taut?

Electronic Devices

Electronic devices use electrical energy. But they do not use electrical energy in the same way that machines do.

Some machines can change electrical energy into other forms of energy in order to do work. Electronic devices use it to handle information.

Inside an Electronic Device

For example, a remote control sends information to a television. **Figure 1** shows the inside of a remote control. The large green board is a circuit board. A **circuit board** is a collection of many circuit parts on a sheet of insulating material. A circuit board connects the parts of the circuit to supply electric current and send signals to the parts of an electronic device.

Sending Information to Your Television

To change the channel or volume on the television, you push buttons on the remote control. When you push a button, you send a signal to the circuit board. The components of the circuit board process the signal to send the correct information to the television. The information is sent to the television in the form of infrared light by a tiny bulb called a *light-emitting diode* (DIE OHD), or LED. In this section, you'll learn about diodes and other components and learn about how they work.

circuit board a sheet of insulating material that carries circuit elements and that is inserted in an electronic device

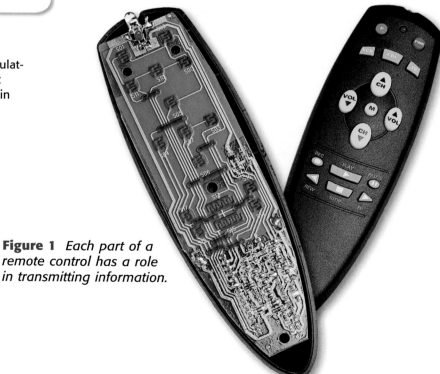

Figure 1 *Each part of a remote control has a role in transmitting information.*

Semiconductors

Semiconductors (SEM i kuhn DUHK tuhrz) are used in many electronic components. A **semiconductor** is a substance that conducts an electric current better than an insulator does but not as well as a conductor does. Semiconductors have allowed people to make incredible advances in electronic technology.

How Do Semiconductors Work?

The way a semiconductor conducts electric current is based on how its electrons are arranged. Silicon, Si, is a widely used semiconductor. As shown in **Figure 2,** when silicon atoms bond, they share all of their valence electrons. There are no electrons free to make much electric current. So, why are semiconductors such as silicon used? They are used because their conductivity can be changed.

Doping

You can change the conductivity of a semiconductor through doping (DOHP eeng). **Doping** is the addition of an impurity to a semiconductor. Adding the impurity changes the arrangement of electrons. A few atoms of the semiconductor are replaced with a few atoms of another element that has a different number of electrons, as shown in **Figure 3.**

✓**Reading Check** What is the result of doping a semiconductor? (*See the Appendix for answers to Reading Checks.*)

Figure 2 *Each silicon atom shares its four valence electrons with other silicon atoms.*

semiconductor an element or compound that conducts electric current better than an insulator does but not as well as a conductor does

doping the addition of an impurity element to a semiconductor

---

Figure 3 Types of Doped Semiconductors

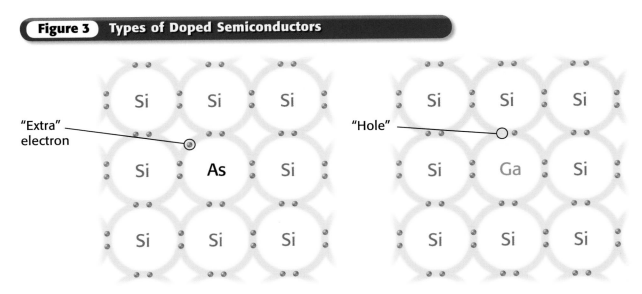

"Extra" electron

"Hole"

N-Type Semiconductor An atom of arsenic, As, has five electrons in its outermost energy level. Replacing a silicon atom with an arsenic atom results in an "extra" electron.

P-Type Semiconductor An atom of gallium, Ga, has three electrons in its outermost energy level. Replacing a silicon atom with a gallium atom results in a "hole" where an electron could be.

Diodes

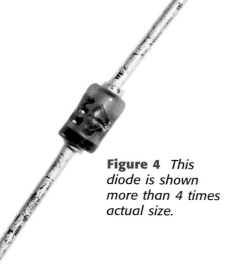

Figure 4 *This diode is shown more than 4 times actual size.*

Layers of semiconductors can be put together like sandwiches to make electronic components. Joining an n-type semiconductor with a p-type semiconductor forms a diode. A **diode** is an electronic component that allows electric charge to move mainly in one direction. Look at **Figure 4.** Each wire joins to one of the layers in the diode.

The Flow of Electrons in Diodes

Where the two layers in a diode meet, some "extra" electrons move from the n-type layer to fill some "holes" in the p-type layer. This change gives the n-type layer a positive charge and the p-type layer a negative charge. If a diode is connected to a source of electrical energy, such as a battery, so that the positive terminal is closer to the p-type layer, a current is made. If the connections are switched so that the negative terminal is closer to the p-type layer, there is no current. **Figure 5** shows how a diode works.

diode an electronic device that allows electric charge to move more easily in one direction than in the other

Using Diodes to Change AC to DC

Power plants send electrical energy to homes by means of alternating current (AC). But many things, such as radios, use direct current (DC). Diodes can help change AC to DC. Alternating current switches direction many times each second. The diodes in an AC adapter block the current in one direction. Other components average the current in the direction that remains. As a result, AC is changed to DC.

✓ **Reading Check** Why can a diode change AC to DC?

Figure 5 How a Diode Works

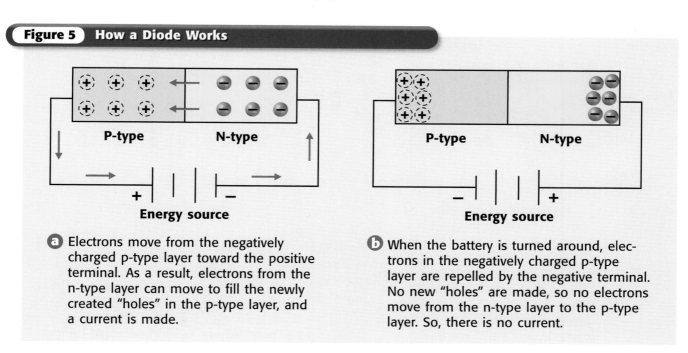

ⓐ Electrons move from the negatively charged p-type layer toward the positive terminal. As a result, electrons from the n-type layer can move to fill the newly created "holes" in the p-type layer, and a current is made.

ⓑ When the battery is turned around, electrons in the negatively charged p-type layer are repelled by the negative terminal. No new "holes" are made, so no electrons move from the n-type layer to the p-type layer. So, there is no current.

Transistors

What do you get when you sandwich three layers of semiconductors together? You get a transistor! A **transistor** is an electronic component that amplifies, or increases, current. It can be used in many circuits, including an amplifier and a switch. Transistors can be NPN or PNP transistors. An NPN transistor has a p-type layer between two n-type layers. A PNP transistor has an n-type layer between two p-type layers. Look at **Figure 6.** Each wire joins to one of the layers in the transistor.

✓ Reading Check Name two kinds of transistors made from semiconductors.

Transistors as Amplifiers

A microphone does not make a current that is large enough to run a loudspeaker. But a transistor can be used in an amplifier to make a larger current. Look at **Figure 7.** In the circuit, there is a small electric current in the microphone. This current triggers the transistor to allow a larger current in the loudspeaker. The electric current can be larger because of a large source of electrical energy in the loudspeaker side of the circuit.

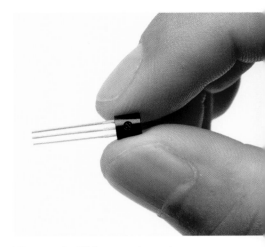

Figure 6 *This transistor is smaller than a pencil eraser!*

transistor a semiconductor device that can amplify current and that is used in amplifiers, oscillators, and switches

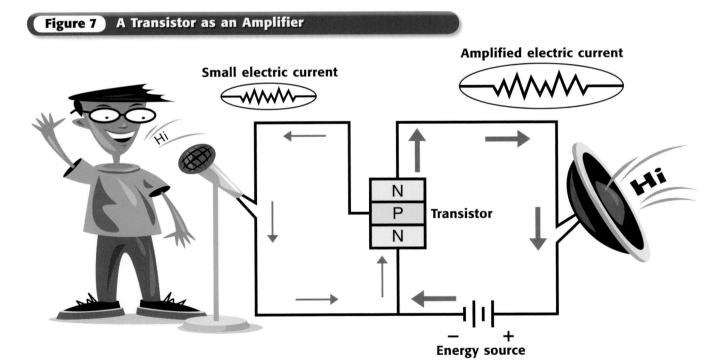

Figure 7 A Transistor as an Amplifier

Small electric current

Amplified electric current

Transistor

Energy source

❶ Sound waves from your voice enter the microphone. As a result, a small electric current is made in the microphone side of the circuit.

❷ A transistor allows the small electric current to control a larger electric current that operates the loudspeaker.

❸ The current in the loudspeaker is larger than the current produced by the microphone. Otherwise, the two currents are identical.

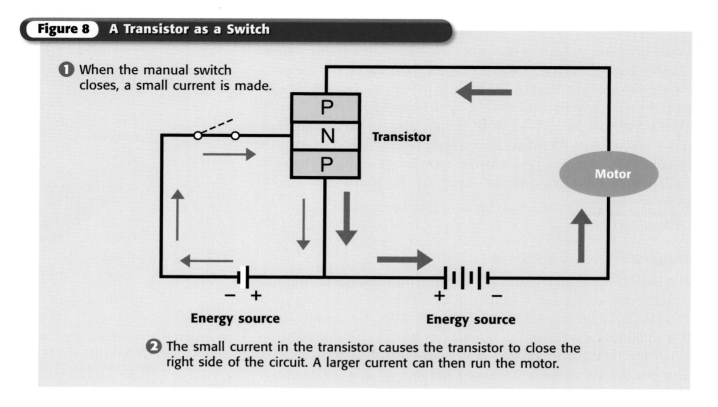

Figure 8 A Transistor as a Switch

❶ When the manual switch closes, a small current is made.

P
N Transistor
P

Motor

− + Energy source

+ − Energy source

❷ The small current in the transistor causes the transistor to close the right side of the circuit. A larger current can then run the motor.

Transistors in Switches

Remote-controlled toy cars use transistors in switches. Look at **Figure 8.** When the manual switch in the circuit is closed, a small current is made in the small loop. The small current causes the transistor to close the large loop on the right. As a result, a larger current is made in the large loop. The larger current runs the motor. You switch on a small current. The transistor switches on a larger current. If the manual switch is opened, the circuit is broken. As a result, the transistor will switch off the current that runs the motor. Computers also rely on transistors that work in switches.

integrated circuit a circuit whose components are formed on a single semiconductor

Integrated Circuits

An **integrated circuit** (IN tuh GRAYT id SUHR kit) is an entire circuit that has many components on a single semiconductor. The parts of the circuit are made by carefully doping certain spots. Look at **Figure 9.** Integrated circuits and circuit boards have helped shrink electronic devices. Many complete circuits can fit into one integrated circuit. So, complicated electronic systems can be made very small. Because the circuits are so small, the electric charges moving through them do not have to travel very far. Devices that use integrated circuits can run at very high speeds.

Figure 9 *This integrated circuit contains many electronic components, yet its dimensions are only about 1 cm × 3 cm!*

✓ **Reading Check** Describe two benefits of using integrated circuits in electronic devices.

Smaller and Smarter Devices

Before transistors and semiconductor diodes were made, vacuum tubes, like the one in **Figure 10,** were used. Vacuum tubes can amplify electric current and change AC to DC. But vacuum tubes are much larger than semiconductor components are. They also get hotter and don't last as long. Early radios had to be large. Space was needed to hold the vacuum tubes and to keep them from overheating. Modern radios are very small. They use transistors and integrated circuits. And your radio might have other features, such as a clock or a CD player. But even more importantly than waking you up to your favorite music, integrated circuits have changed the world through their use in computers.

Figure 10 *Vacuum tubes are much larger than the transistors used today. So, radios that used the tubes were very large also.*

SECTION
Review

Summary

- Circuit boards contain circuits that supply current to different parts of electronic devices.

- Semiconductors are often used in electronic devices because their conductivity can be changed by doping.

- Diodes allow current in one direction and can change AC to DC.

- Transistors are used in amplifiers and switches.

- Integrated circuits have made smaller, smarter electronic devices possible.

Using Key Terms

For each pair of terms, explain how the meanings of the terms differ.

1. *circuit board* and *integrated circuit*

2. *semiconductor* and *doping*

3. *diode* and *transistor*

Understanding Key Ideas

4. Which element forms the basis for semiconductors?
   a. oxygen
   b. gallium
   c. arsenic
   d. silicon

5. Describe how p-type and n-type semiconductors are made.

6. Explain how a diode changes AC to DC.

7. What are two purposes transistors serve?

Math Skills

8. An integrated circuit that was made in 1974 contained 6,000 transistors. An integrated circuit that was made in 2000 contained 42,000,000 transistors. How many times more transistors did the circuit made in 2000 have?

Critical Thinking

9. **Making Comparisons** How might an electronic system that uses vacuum tubes be different from one that uses integrated circuits?

10. **Applying Concepts** Would modern computers be possible without integrated circuits? Explain.

Interpreting Graphics

11. The graph below represents electric current in a series circuit. Does the circuit contain a diode? Explain your reasoning.

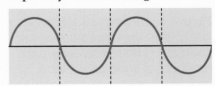

For a variety of links related to this chapter, go to www.scilinks.org

Topic: Transistors
SciLinks code: HSM1550

Developed and maintained by the
National Science Teachers Association

Communication Technology

What electronic devices do you use to send or receive information? Your answer might include telephones, radios, or televisions.

In this section, you'll study these and other electronic devices that are used for communication. You'll also learn about two kinds of signals used to send and store information.

Communicating with Signals

One of the first electronic communication devices was the telegraph. It was invented in the 1830s. It used an electric current to send messages between places joined by wires. People sent messages in Morse code through the wires. **Table 1** shows the patterns of dots and dashes that stand for each letter and number in Morse code. The message was sent by tapping a telegraph key, like the one in **Figure 1.** This tapping closed a circuit, causing "clicks" at the receiving end of the telegraph.

Signals and Carriers

Electronic communication devices, including the telegraph, send information by using signals. A *signal* is anything, such as a movement, a sound, or a set of numbers and letters, that can be used to send information. Often, one signal is sent using another signal called a *carrier*. Electric current is the carrier of the signals made by tapping a telegraph key. Two kinds of signals are analog signals and digital signals.

READING WARM-UP

Objectives

- Identify how signals transmit information.
- Describe analog signals and their use in telephones and records.
- Describe digital signals and their use in compact discs.
- Describe how information is transmitted and received in radios and televisions.

Terms to Learn

analog signal
digital signal

READING STRATEGY

Discussion Read this section silently. Write down questions that you have about this section. Discuss your questions in a small group.

Figure 1 *By tapping this telegraph key in the right combinations of short taps (dots) and long taps (dashes), people could send messages over long distances.*

Table 1	International Morse Code						
A	·—	G	—·—	Q	————	1	·————
B	—····	H	····	R	·—·	2	··———
C	————	I	··	S	···	3	···——
D	—··	J	·———	T	—	4	····—
E	·	K	—·—	U	··—	5	·····
F	··—·	L	·—··	V	···—	6	—····
		M	——	W	·——	7	——···
		N	—·	X	—··—	8	———··
		O	———	Y	—·——	9	————·
		P	·——·	Z	——··	0	—————

Analog Signals

An **analog signal** (AN uh LAWG SIG nuhl) is a signal whose properties change without a break or jump between values. Think of a dimmer switch on a light. You can continuously change the brightness of the light using the dimmer switch.

The changes in an analog signal are based on changes in the original information. For example, when you talk on the phone, the sound of your voice is changed into changing electric current in the form of a wave. This wave is an analog signal that is similar to the original sound wave. But remember that sound waves do not travel down your phone line!

✓ **Reading Check** What is an analog signal? (*See the Appendix for answers to Reading Checks.*)

Talking on the Phone

Look at the telephone in **Figure 2.** You talk into the transmitter. You listen to the receiver. The transmitter changes the sound waves made when you speak into an analog signal. This signal moves through phone wires to the receiver of another phone. The receiver changes the analog signal back into the sound of your voice. Sometimes, the analog signals are changed to digital signals and back again before they reach the other person. You will learn about digital signals later in this section.

analog signal a signal whose properties can change continuously in a given range

CONNECTION TO Geology

Seismograms A *seismograph* is a device used by scientists to record waves made by earthquakes. It makes a *seismogram*—wavy lines on paper that record ground movement. Draw an example of a seismogram that shows changes in the wave, and explain why this is an example of an analog signal.

ACTIVITY

Figure 2 How a Telephone Works

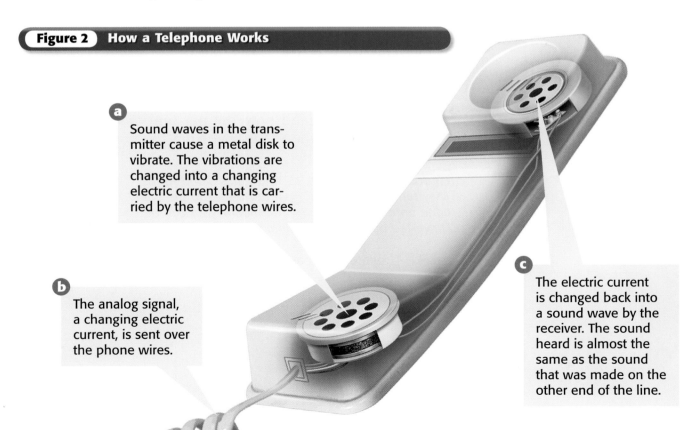

a Sound waves in the transmitter cause a metal disk to vibrate. The vibrations are changed into a changing electric current that is carried by the telephone wires.

b The analog signal, a changing electric current, is sent over the phone wires.

c The electric current is changed back into a sound wave by the receiver. The sound heard is almost the same as the sound that was made on the other end of the line.

Analog Recording

If you want to save a sound, you can store an analog signal of the sound wave. In vinyl records, the signal is made into grooves on a plastic disk. The sound's properties are represented by the number and depth of the contours in the disk.

Playing a Record

Figure 3 shows a record being played. The stylus (STIE luhs), or needle, makes an electromagnet vibrate. The vibrating electromagnet induces an electric current that is used to make sound. Analog recording makes sound that is very close to the original. But unwanted sounds are sometimes recorded and are not easy to remove. Also, the stylus touches the record to play it. So, the record wears out, and the sound changes over time.

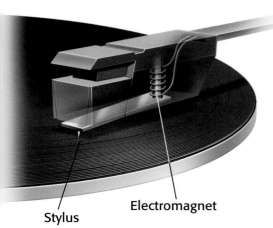

Stylus
Electromagnet

Figure 3 *As the stylus rides in the record's grooves, it causes an electromagnet to vibrate.*

digital signal a signal that can be represented as a sequence of discrete values

Digital Signals

A **digital signal** is a signal that is represented as a sequence of separate values. It does not change continuously. Think of a regular light switch. It can be either on or off. Information in a digital signal is represented as binary (BIE nuh ree) numbers. *Binary* means "two." Numbers in binary are made up of only two digits, 1 and 0. Each digit is a *bit,* which is short for *binary digit.* Computers process digital signals that are in the form of a pattern of electric pulses. Each pulse stands for a 1. Each missing pulse stands for a 0.

Digital Storage on a CD

You've probably heard digital sound from a compact disc, or CD. Sound is recorded to a CD by means of a digital signal. A CD stores the signals in a thin layer of aluminum. Look at **Figure 4.** To understand how the pits and lands are named, keep in mind that the CD is read from the bottom.

Figure 4 *Pits stand for 1s, and lands stand for 0s. They form a tight spiral from the center to the outer edge on a CD. They store information that can be converted by a CD player into sound.*

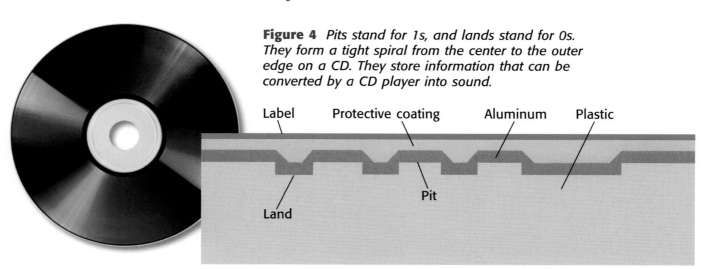

Label   Protective coating   Aluminum   Plastic

Land   Pit

Digital Recording

In a digital recording, the sound wave is measured many times each second. **Figure 5** shows how these sample values represent the original sound. These numbers are then changed into binary values using 1s and 0s. The 1s and 0s are stored as pits and lands on a CD.

In digital recording, the sample values don't exactly match the original sound wave. So, the number of samples taken each second is important to make sure the recording sounds the way it should sound. Taking more sample values each second makes a digital sound that is closer to the original sound.

✓ Reading Check How can a digital recording be made to sound more like the original sound?

Playing a CD

In a CD player, the CD spins around while a laser shines on the CD from below. As shown in **Figure 6,** light reflected from the CD enters a detector. The detector changes the pattern of light and dark into a digital signal. The digital signal is changed into an analog signal, which is used to make a sound wave. Because only light touches the CD, the CD doesn't wear out. But errors can happen from playing a dirty or scratched CD.

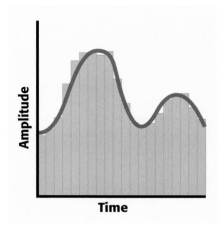

Figure 5 *Each of the bars represent a digital sample of the sound wave.*

Figure 6 **How a CD Player Works**

Different sequences and sizes of pits and lands will register different patterns of numbers that are converted into different sounds.

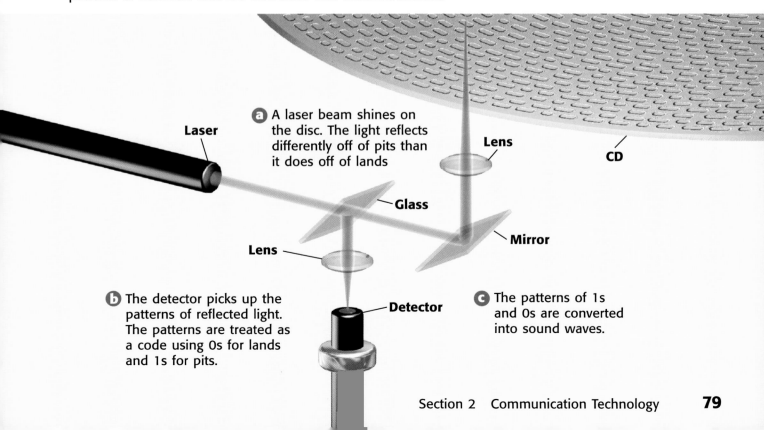

Laser

a A laser beam shines on the disc. The light reflects differently off of pits than it does off of lands

Lens

CD

Glass

Lens

Mirror

b The detector picks up the patterns of reflected light. The patterns are treated as a code using 0s for lands and 1s for pits.

Detector

c The patterns of 1s and 0s are converted into sound waves.

Radio and Television

You hear or see shows on your radio or television that are broadcast from a station that may be many kilometers away. The radio and TV signals can be either analog or digital. An *electromagnetic* (EM) *wave* is a wave that consists of changing electric and magnetic fields. EM waves are used as carriers.

Radio

Radio waves are one kind of EM wave. Radio stations use radio waves to carry signals that represent sound. Look at **Figure 7**. Radio waves are transmitted by a radio tower. They travel through the air and are picked up by a radio antenna.

INTERNET ACTIVITY

For another activity related to this chapter, go to **go.hrw.com** and type in the keyword **HP5ELTW.**

Figure 7 How a Radio Works

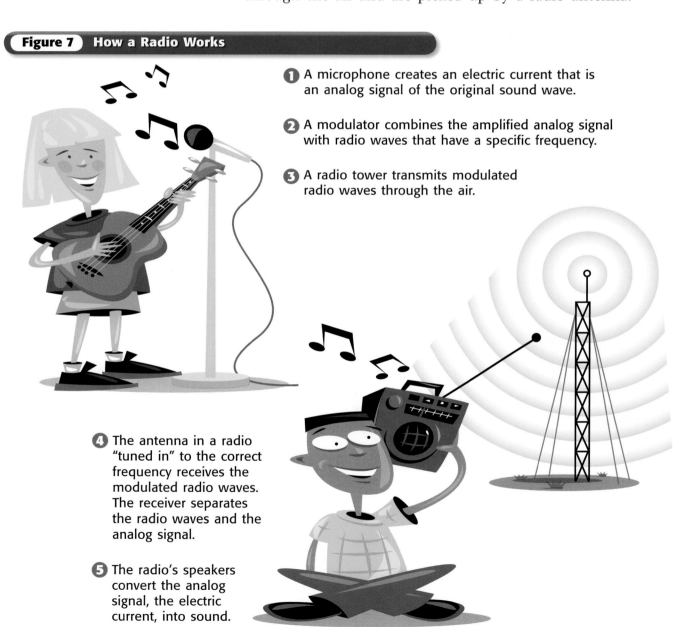

❶ A microphone creates an electric current that is an analog signal of the original sound wave.

❷ A modulator combines the amplified analog signal with radio waves that have a specific frequency.

❸ A radio tower transmits modulated radio waves through the air.

❹ The antenna in a radio "tuned in" to the correct frequency receives the modulated radio waves. The receiver separates the radio waves and the analog signal.

❺ The radio's speakers convert the analog signal, the electric current, into sound.

Television

The pictures you see on your television are made by beams of electrons hitting the screen, as described in **Figure 8.** Video signals hold the information to make a picture. Audio signals hold the information to make the sound. These signals can be sent as analog or digital signals to your television. The signals can be broadcast using EM waves as carriers. The signals can be sent through cables or from satellites or broadcast towers.

More and more, television programs are going digital. This means that they are filmed using digital cameras and transmitted to homes as digital signals. You can watch digital shows on an analog TV. However, on a digital display, the images and sound of these programs are much clearer than on a television made for analog broadcasts.

Reading Check What kinds of signals can be picked up by a color television?

TV Screen

With an adult, use a magnifying lens to look at a television screen. How are the fluorescent materials arranged? Hold the lens at various distances from the screen. What effects do you see? How does the screen's changing picture affect what you see?

ACTIVITY

Figure 8 **Images on a Color Television**

1 Video signals transmitted from a TV station are received by the antenna of a TV receiver.

2 Electronic circuits divide the video signal into separate signals for each of three electron beams. The beams, one for each primary color of light (red, green, and blue), strike the screen in varying strengths determined by the video signal.

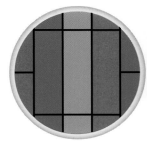

3 The screen has stripes or dots of three fluorescent (FLOO uh RES uhnt) materials. These materials glow when hit by electrons. The electron beams sweep the screen 30 times every second and activate the fluorescent materials. These materials then emit colored light that is viewed as a picture.

Plasma Display

Standard televisions must be deep enough so that the electron beams can reach all parts of the screen. So, televisions are bulky and heavy. A newer kind of screen, called a *plasma display,* is much thinner. It can be as thin as 15 cm. So, it is not much thicker than a painting on the wall!

Figure 9 shows how a plasma display works. Plasma displays do not use electron tubes. Instead, they have thousands of tiny cells with gases in them. A computer charges the cells, making a current in the gases. The current generates colored lights. Each light can be red, green, blue, or a combination. As in a regular television, these three colors are combined to make every picture on the screen.

✓ Reading Check Why is a plasma display thinner than a regular television?

Figure 9 How a Plasma Display Works

❶ Video signals transmitted from a TV station are received by a device, such as a VCR, that has a television tuner in it. The signals are then sent to the plasma display.

❷ The signal includes commands to charge conductors on either side of small wells in the screen. The atoms of gas in the wells become charged and form a plasma.

❸ Each well contains one of three fluorescent materials. The materials give off red, blue, or green light after absorbing energy given off by the plasma.

❹ The colored light from each group of three wells blends together and makes a small dot of light in the picture on the screen.

Summary

- Signals transmit information in electronic devices. Signals can be transmitted using a carrier. Signals can be analog or digital.

- Analog signals have continuous values. Telephones, record players, radios, and regular TV sets use analog signals.

- In a telephone, a transmitter changes sound waves to electric current. The current is sent across a phone line. The receiving telephone converts the signal back into a sound wave.

- Analog signals of sounds are used to make vinyl records. Changes in the groove reflect changes in the sound.

- Digital signals have discrete values, such as 0 and 1. CD players use digital signals.

- Radios and televisions use electromagnetic waves. These waves travel through the atmosphere. In a radio, the signals are converted to sound waves. In a television, electron beams convert the signals into images on the screen.

Using Key Terms

1. In your own words, write a definition for each of the following terms: *analog signal* and *digital signal*.

Understanding Key Ideas

2. Which of the following objects changes sound waves into an electric current in order to transmit information?
   - **a.** telephone
   - **b.** radio
   - **c.** television
   - **d.** telegraph

3. Why are carriers used to transmit signals?

4. What is an early example of an electrical device used for sending information over long distances? How did this device work?

Critical Thinking

5. **Applying Concepts** Is Morse code an example of an analog signal or a digital signal? Explain your reasoning.

6. **Making Comparisons** Compare how a telephone and a radio tower transmit information.

7. **Making Inferences** Does a mercury thermometer provide information in an analog or digital way? Explain your reasoning.

Interpreting Graphics

8. Look at the graphs below. They represent a sound wave that is being changed into a digital signal. Each bar represents a digital sample of the sound wave. Which graph represents the digital signal that is closer to the original sound wave? Explain your reasoning.

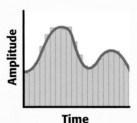

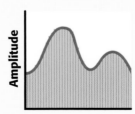

For a variety of links related to this chapter, go to www.scilinks.org

Topic: Telephone Technology; Television Technology

SciLinks code: HSM1499; HSM1501

Computers

Did you use a computer to wake up this morning?

You might think of a computer as something you use to send e-mail or to surf the Internet. But computers are around you all the time. Computers are in automobiles, VCRs, and telephones. Even an alarm clock is an example of a simple computer!

What Is a Computer?

A **computer** is an electronic device that performs tasks by following instructions given to it. A computer does a task when it is given a command and has the instructions necessary to carry out that command. Computers can do tasks very quickly.

Basic Functions

The basic functions of a computer are shown in **Figure 1.** The information you give to a computer is called *input.* The computer *processes* the input. Processing could mean adding a list of numbers, making a drawing, or even moving a piece of equipment. Input doesn't have to be processed right away. It can be stored until it is needed. The computer *stores* information in its memory. *Output* is the final result of the job done by the computer.

✔ **Reading Check** What are the basic functions of a computer? (*See the Appendix for answers to Reading Checks.*)

READING WARM-UP

Objectives

- List a computer's basic functions, and describe its development.
- Identify the main components of computer hardware.
- Explain how information can be stored on CD-Rs and CD-RWs.
- Describe what computer software allows a computer to do.
- Describe computer networks.

Terms to Learn

computer   software
microprocessor   Internet
hardware

READING STRATEGY

Prediction Guide Before reading this section, write the title of each heading in this section. Next, under each heading, write what you think you will learn.

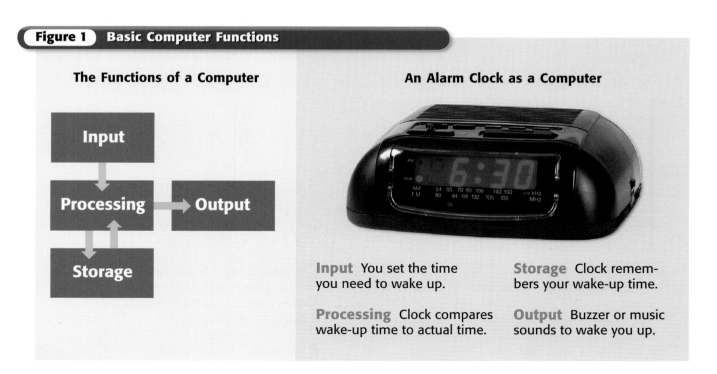

Figure 1 Basic Computer Functions

The Functions of a Computer

Input → Processing → Output

Processing ⇄ Storage

An Alarm Clock as a Computer

Input You set the time you need to wake up.

Processing Clock compares wake-up time to actual time.

Storage Clock remembers your wake-up time.

Output Buzzer or music sounds to wake you up.

The First Computers

Your pocket calculator is a simple computer. But computers were not always so small and easy to use. The first computers were huge! They were made up of large pieces of equipment that could fill a room. The first general-purpose computer is shown in **Figure 2.** This is the ENIAC. ENIAC stands for Electronic Numerical Integrator and Computer. It was made in 1946 by the U.S. Army. The ENIAC was made up of thousands of vacuum tubes. As a result, it had to be cooled while in use. It also cost a lot to build and to run.

Figure 2 *Fast for its time, the ENIAC could add 5,000 numbers per second.*

Modern Computers

Computers have become much smaller because of integrated circuits. Computers today use microprocessors. A **microprocessor** is a single chip that controls and carries out a computer's instructions. The first widely available microprocessor had only 4,800 transistors. But microprocessors made today may have more than 40 million transistors. Computers are now made so small that we can carry them around like a book!

computer an electronic device that can accept data and instructions, follow the instructions, and output the results

microprocessor a single semi-conductor chip that controls and executes a microcomputer's instructions

✓ **Reading Check** What is a microprocessor?

The Speed of a Simple Computer

1. With a partner, use a **clock** to measure the time it takes each of you to solve the following items by hand.
   a. (108 ÷ 9) + 231 − 19
   b. 1 × 2 × 3 × 4 × 5
   c. (4 × 6 × 8) ÷ 2
   d. 3 × (5 + 12) − 2
2. Repeat step 1 using a **calculator.**
3. Which method was faster?
4. Which method was more accurate?
5. Will the calculator always give you the correct answer? Explain.

Computer Hardware

Different parts of a computer do different jobs. **Hardware** is the parts or pieces of equipment that make up a computer. As you read about each piece of hardware, look at **Figure 3** and **Figure 4** to see what the hardware looks like.

hardware the parts or pieces of equipment that make up a computer

Input Devices

An *input device* gives information, or input, to the computer. You can enter information into a computer using a keyboard, a mouse, a scanner, or a digitizing pad and pen. You can even enter information using a microphone.

Central Processing Unit

A computer does tasks in the *central processing unit,* or CPU. In a personal computer, the CPU is a microprocessor. Input goes through the CPU for processing on the spot or for storage in memory. In the CPU, the computer does calculations, solves problems, and carries out instructions given to it.

✓ *Reading Check* What does *CPU* stand for?

CONNECTION TO
Social Studies

WRITING SKILL **ENIAC** ENIAC was developed for use by the U.S. Army during World War II. Research what ENIAC was to be used for in the war and what plans were made for ENIAC after the war. Write a one-page report in your **science journal** to report your findings.

Figure 3 Computer Hardware

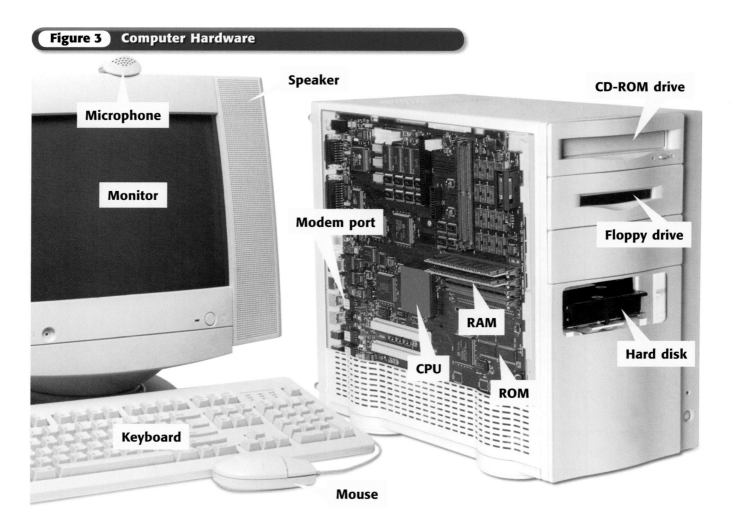

Microphone
Speaker
CD-ROM drive
Monitor
Modem port
Floppy drive
RAM
CPU
ROM
Hard disk
Keyboard
Mouse

Memory

Information can be stored in the computer's memory until it is needed. Hard disks inside a computer and floppy disks or CDs that are put into a computer have memory to store information. Two other types of memory are *ROM* (read-only memory) and *RAM* (random-access memory).

ROM is permanent. It handles jobs such as start-up, maintenance, and hardware management. ROM normally cannot be added to or changed. It also cannot be lost when the computer is turned off. RAM is temporary. RAM stores information only while it is being used. RAM is sometimes called *working memory*. Information in RAM is lost if the power is shut off. So, it is a good habit to save your work to a hard drive or to a disk every few minutes.

Output Devices

Once a computer does a job, it shows the results on an *output device*. Monitors, printers, and speaker systems are all examples of output devices.

Modems and Interface Cards

Computers can exchange information if they are joined by modems or interface cards. Modems send information through telephone lines. Modems convert information from a digital signal to an analog signal and vice versa. Interface cards use cables or wireless connections.

Computer Memory

Suppose you download a document from the Internet that uses 25 kilobytes of memory. How many of those documents could you fit on a disk that has 1 gigabyte of memory? A kilobyte is 1,024 bytes, and a gigabyte is 1,073,741,824 bytes.

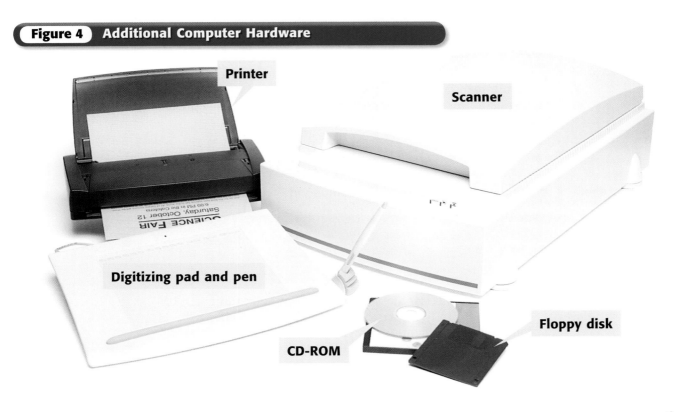

Figure 4 Additional Computer Hardware

Printer

Scanner

Digitizing pad and pen

CD-ROM

Floppy disk

Compact Discs

Today, you can use a CD burner to make your own compact discs. A CD can hold about 500 times more information than a floppy disk. It can store digital photos, music files, and any other type of computer file.

Burning and Erasing CDs

The first kind of CD that you could put information onto, or "burn," is a CD-recordable (CD-R) disc. CD-R discs use a dye to block light. When the dye is heated, light cannot pass through to reflect off the aluminum. To burn a CD, a special laser heats some places and not others. This burning creates a pattern of "on" and "off" spots on the CD-R. These spots store information just as the pits and lands do on a regular CD. You can burn a CD-R disc only once.

A CD-rewritable (CD-RW) disc can be used more than once. CD-RW discs use a special compound that can be erased and written over again. CD-RW discs cost more than CD-R discs. But CD-RW discs cannot be read by all CD players. Look at **Figure 5** to see how CD-R and CD-RW discs work.

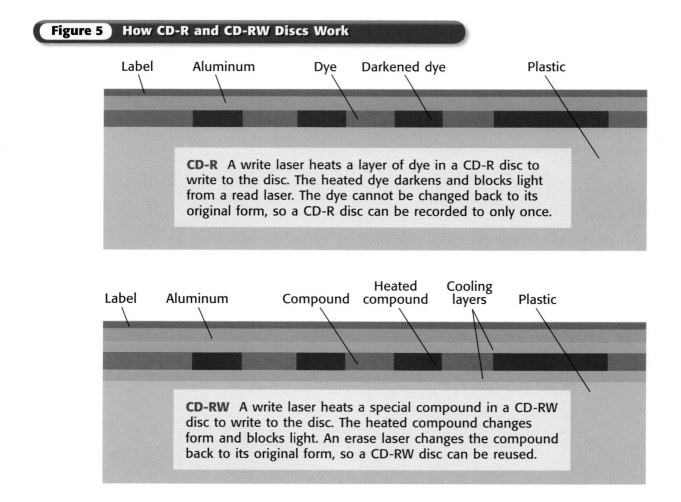

Figure 5 How CD-R and CD-RW Discs Work

Label Aluminum Dye Darkened dye Plastic

CD-R A write laser heats a layer of dye in a CD-R disc to write to the disc. The heated dye darkens and blocks light from a read laser. The dye cannot be changed back to its original form, so a CD-R disc can be recorded to only once.

Label Aluminum Compound Heated compound Cooling layers Plastic

CD-RW A write laser heats a special compound in a CD-RW disc to write to the disc. The heated compound changes form and blocks light. An erase laser changes the compound back to its original form, so a CD-RW disc can be reused.

Computer Software

Computers need instructions before they can do any given task. **Software** is a set of instructions or commands that tells a computer what to do. A computer program is software.

software a set of instructions or commands that tells a computer what to do; a computer program

Kinds of Software

Software can be split into two kinds: operating-system software and application software. Operating-system software handles basic operations needed by the computer. It helps the software and hardware communicate. It also handles commands from an input device. It can find programming instructions on a hard disk to be loaded into memory.

Application software tells the computer to run a utility, such as the ones shown in **Figure 6.** The pages in this book were made using many kinds of application software!

✓ **Reading Check** What are the two main kinds of software?

Figure 6 **Common Types of Computer Software**

Word Processing

Video Games

Interactive Instruction

Graphics

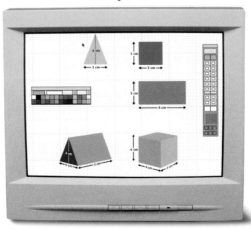

Computer Networks

By using modems and software, many computers can be connected, which allows them to communicate with one another. The **Internet** is a huge computer network made up of millions of computers that can all share information.

The Internet

Figure 7 shows some ways computers can be connected. Computers can connect on the Internet by using modems to dial into an Internet Service Provider, or ISP. A home computer often connects to an ISP over a phone or cable line. Computers in a school or business can be joined in a Local Area Network, or LAN. These computers connect to an ISP through only one line. ISPs around the world are connected by fiber optic cables.

The World Wide Web

The part of the Internet that people know best is called the *World Wide Web.* When you use a Web browser to look at pages on the Internet, you are on the World Wide Web. Web pages share a format that is simple enough that any computer can view them. They are grouped into Web sites. Clicking on a link takes you from one page or site to another. You can use a search engine to find Web pages on a topic for a report or to find out about your favorite movie!

✓ **Reading Check** Describe the World Wide Web.

Internet a large computer network that connects many local and smaller networks all over the world

Figure 7 *Internet Service Providers allow computers in your home or school to connect to large routing computers that are linked around the world.*

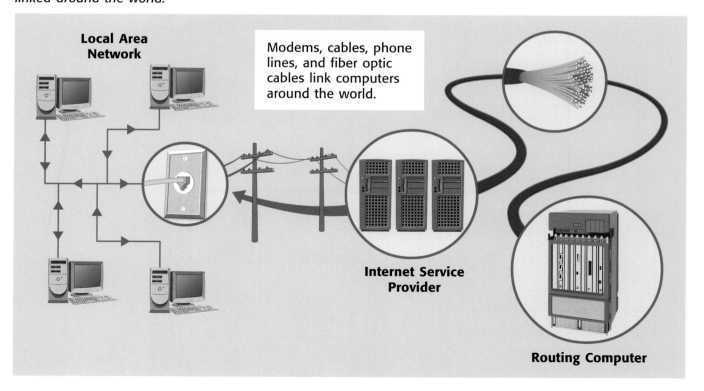

Local Area Network

Modems, cables, phone lines, and fiber optic cables link computers around the world.

Internet Service Provider

Routing Computer

Summary

● All computers have four basic functions: input, processing, storage, and output.

● The first general-purpose computer, ENIAC, was made of thousands of vacuum tubes and filled an entire room. Microprocessors have made it possible to have computers the size of notebooks.

● Computer hardware includes input devices, the CPU, memory, output devices, and modems.

● CD burners can store information on recordable CDs, or CD-Rs. Rewritable CDs, or CD-RWs, can be erased and reused. Both use patterns of light and dark spots.

● Computer software is a set of instructions that tell a computer what to do. The two main types are operating systems and applications. Applications include word processors, spreadsheets, and games.

● The Internet is a huge network that allows millions of computers to share information.

Using Key Terms

The statements below are false. For each statement, replace the underlined term to make a true statement.

1. A word-processing application is an example of <u>hardware</u>.

2. An ISP allows you to connect to the <u>microprocessor</u>.

Understanding Key Ideas

3. Which of the following is an example of hardware used for input?
   a. monitor   **c.** printer
   b. keyboard   **d.** speaker

4. How are modern computers different from ENIAC? How are they the same?

5. What is the difference between hardware and software?

6. Explain how a CD burner works.

7. What is the Internet?

Critical Thinking

8. **Applying Concepts** Using the terms *input, output, processing,* and *store,* explain how you use a pocket calculator to add numbers.

9. **Predicting Consequences** If no phone lines were working, would there be any communication on the Internet? Explain.

Math Skills

10. How many 800 KB digital photos could you burn onto a CD-R disc that can hold 700 MB of information? (Note: 1,024 KB = 1 MB)

Interpreting Graphics

11. Look at the image of a RAM module below. Each of the black rectangles on the module is 32 MB of RAM. Each side of the module has the same number of rectangles. How much total RAM does the module have?

For a variety of links related to this chapter, go to www.scilinks.org

Topic: Computer Technology; Internet
SciLinks code: HSM0334; HSM0808

Skills Practice Lab

Sending Signals

OBJECTIVES

Build a working model of a telegraph key.

Send a message in Morse code by using your model.

Receive a message in Morse code by using your model.

MATERIALS

- battery, 6 V
- flashlight bulb with bulb holder
- paper clip (3)
- thumbtack (2)
- wire, insulated, with ends stripped, 15 cm (4)
- wood block, small

SAFETY

With a telegraph, you can use electric current to send signals between two telegraph keys connected by wires. In this lab, you will build a model of a telegraph that allows you to use Morse code to transmit messages to a friend.

Procedure

1. Build a switch on the wood block, as shown below. Use a thumbtack to tack down a paper clip so that one end of the paper clip hangs over the edge of the wood block.

2. Unfold a second paper clip so that it looks like an *s*. Use the second thumbtack to tack down one end of the open paper clip on top of the remaining paper clip. The free end of the closed paper clip should hang off of the edge of the wood block opposite the first paper clip. The free end of the open paper clip should touch the thumbtack below it when pushed down.

3. Build the rest of the circuit, as shown below. Use a wire to connect one terminal of the battery to one of the paper clips that hangs over the edge of the wood block.

4. Use a second wire to connect the other paper clip that hangs over the edge of the wood block to the bulb holder.

5. Use a third wire to connect the other side of the bulb holder with the second terminal of the battery.

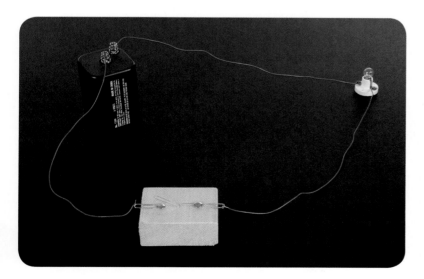

6. Test your circuit by gently pressing down on the open paper clip so that it touches the thumbtack below it. The light bulb should light. This is your model of a telegraph key.

7. Connect your model to another team's model. Use the remaining wire in each team's materials to connect the bulb holders, as shown on the next page. Test your circuit by closing each switch one at a time.

⑧ Write a short, four- or five-word message in Morse code. Take turns sending messages to the other team using the telegraph. To send a dot, press the paper clip down for two seconds. To send a dash, hold the clip down for four seconds. Decode the message you receive, and check to see if you got the correct message.

⑨ Remove one of the batteries. Test your circuit again by closing each switch one at a time.

Analyze the Results

① **Describing Events** When both batteries are attached, what happens to the flashlight bulbs when you close your switch?

② **Describing Events** When both batteries are attached, what happens to the flashlight bulbs when the other team closes their switch?

③ **Describing Events** How does removing one of the batteries change the way you can send or receive messages on the telegraph?

④ **Analyzing Results** Did you receive the correct message from the other team? If not, what problems did you have?

Draw Conclusions

⑤ **Drawing Conclusions** When the two models are connected, are the flashlight bulbs part of a series circuit or a parallel circuit?

⑥ **Making Predictions** How might using a telegraph to transmit messages overseas be difficult?

Table 1	International Morse Code		
A ·–	J ·–––	S ···	2 ··–––
B –···	K –·–	T –	3 ···––
C –·–·	L ·–··	U ··–	4 ····–
D –··	M ––	V ···–	5 ·····
E ·	N –·	W ·––	6 –····
F ··–·	O –––	X –··–	7 ––···
G ––·	P ·––·	Y –·––	8 –––··
H ····	Q ––·–	Z ––··	9 ––––·
I ··	R ·–·	1 ·––––	0 –––––

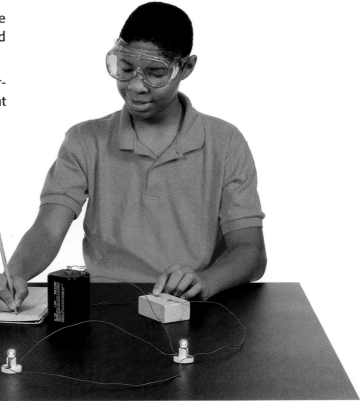

Chapter Review

USING KEY TERMS

For each pair of terms, explain how the meanings of the terms differ.

1 *semiconductor* and *integrated circuit*

2 *transistor* and *doping*

3 *analog signal* and *digital signal*

4 *computer* and *microprocessor*

5 *hardware* and *software*

UNDERSTANDING KEY IDEAS

Multiple Choice

6 All electronic devices transmit information using
  a. signals.
  b. electromagnetic waves.
  c. radio waves.
  d. modems.

7 Semiconductors are used to make
  a. transistors.
  b. integrated circuits.
  c. diodes.
  d. All of the above

8 Which of the following is an example of a telecommunication device?
  a. vacuum tube
  b. telephone
  c. radio
  d. Both (b) and (c)

9 A monitor, a printer, and a speaker are examples of
  a. input devices.
  b. memory.
  c. computers.
  d. output devices.

10 Record players play sounds that were recorded in the form of
  a. digital signals.
  b. electric currents.
  c. analog signals.
  d. radio waves.

11 Memory in a computer that is permanent and cannot be changed is called
  a. RAM.
  b. ROM.
  c. CPU.
  d. None of the above

12 Beams of electrons that shine on fluorescent materials are used in
  a. telephones.
  b. telegraphs.
  c. televisions.
  d. radios.

Short Answer

13 How is an electronic device different from other machines that use electrical energy?

14 In one or two sentences, describe how a television works.

15 Give three examples of how computers are used in your everyday life.

16 Explain the advantages that transistors have over vacuum tubes.

Math Skills

17 How many bits can be stored on a 20 GB hard disk? (Hint: 1 GB = 1,073,741,824 bytes; 1 byte = 8 bits.)

CRITICAL THINKING

18 **Concept Mapping** Use the following terms to create a concept map: *electronic devices, radio waves, electric current, signals,* and *information.*

19 **Applying Concepts** Your friend is preparing an oral report on the history of radio and finds the photograph shown below. He asks you why the radio is so large. Using what you know about electronic devices, how do you explain the size of this vintage radio?

20 **Making Comparisons** Using what you know about the differences between analog signals and digital signals, compare the sound from a record player to the sound from a CD player.

21 **Making Comparisons** What do Morse code and digital signals have in common?

INTERPRETING GRAPHICS

The diagram below shows a circuit that contains a transistor. Use the diagram below to answer the questions that follow.

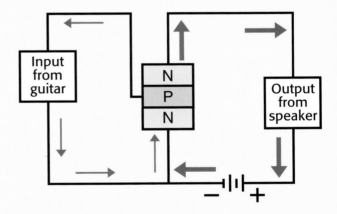

22 What purpose does the transistor serve in this diagram?

23 Compare the current in the left side of the circuit with the current in the right side of the circuit.

24 Compare the sound from the speaker with the sound from the guitar.

READING

Read each of the passages below. Then, answer the questions that follow each passage.

Passage 1 The first televisions hit the market in the 1940s. At about $625 each, they were too expensive for most families to afford. Although the sets were large and bulky, the screens were small, and images were fuzzy and in black and white. Today's televisions have bigger screens and sharper pictures—in full color. Modern televisions are also generally less expensive. A typical television today costs less than half what it cost in the 1940s, and that cost is not accounting for inflation. Many modern televisions are cable ready and have remote controls. You can buy televisions with built-in DVD or videotape players. You could even install theater-quality surround sound. But even these improvements may seem out of date in 20 years.

1. Which of the following can be inferred from the passage?
   A Color movies are better than black-and-white movies.
   B In the 1940s, television sets did not have remote controls.
   C Today's televisions are not much better than the TVs made in the 1940s.
   D Televisions are much more expensive today than they were in the past.

2. Which of the following statements is a fact in the passage?
   F The first television sets had small screens with fuzzy, black-and-white images.
   G Televisions with built-in videotape players are very expensive.
   H Television screens are too large.
   I Although televisions are improving, the quality of TV programming is getting worse.

Passage 2 One of the first electronic communication devices was the telegraph, which was invented in the 1830s. The telegraph used an electric current to send messages between two distant places linked by wires. Telegraph operators sent messages in Morse code, which uses combinations of short taps and long taps to represent numbers and letters. When operators tapped the telegraph key, this closed a circuit, causing "clicks" at the receiving end of the telegraph. Although telegraphs are not used much today, they were an important step in the development of electronic telecommunication.

1. What is the meaning of the word *telecommunication* in this passage?
   A using telephones to communicate
   B sending messages to someone within hearing distance
   C trying to decipher codes without a key
   D communicating with someone over a long distance

2. What happens first when an operator sends a telegraph message?
   F A circuit opens and closes with the pattern of short and long taps.
   G There are short and long clicks on the receiving end.
   H The operator taps the telegraph key with a pattern of short and long taps.
   I The message is deciphered and interpreted by the receiver.

The table below gives the cost of parts to build your own personal computer. Use the table below to answer the questions that follow.

Cost of Computer Parts	
Part	**Cost**
Case	$50–$200
Power supply (300–400 W)	$30–$50
CPU (1.7–2.26 GHz)	$80–$250
Cooling equipment (may come with case)	$0–$50
Motherboard	$50–$200
RAM (256–512 MB)	$50–$150
Floppy drive	$20
Hard drive (60–100 GB)	$80–$125
CD-ROM drive or DVD-ROM drive or CD-RW/DVD combo	$35–$120
Video card	$40–$175
Sound card (may be optional)	$0–$200
Speakers	$10–$150
Microphone (optional)	$0–$50
Keyboard and mouse	$50–$80
Monitor	$200–$600

1. Which of the following items is optional when building a computer?

  A a CPU

  B a hard drive

  C RAM

  D a microphone

2. What is the total cost to purchase the most expensive CPU, the most expensive motherboard, and the least expensive monitor?

  F $330

  G $650

  H $730

  I $1,050

Read each question below, and choose the best answer.

1. A plasma television is 15 cm thick. What is this value in inches? (1 in. = 2.5 cm)

  A 6 in.

  B 12 in.

  C 17.5 in.

  D 37.5 in.

2. The radius of a compact disc is about 6 cm. What is the approximate area of a compact disc? (Estimate the value of π to be 3.)

  F 36 cm

  G 36 cm^2

  H 108 cm

  I 108 cm^2

3. When sound is recorded digitally onto a CD, the sound waves are converted to electric current. The current is sampled about 44,000 times per second to make a digital signal. About how many samples would be taken in 1 min?

  A 733

  B 264,000

  C 733,000

  D 2,640,000

4. The first general-purpose computer, ENIAC, was made of 18,000 vacuum tubes. ENIAC used about 180,000 W of power. About how much power was consumed by each vacuum tube?

  F 0.1 W

  G 1.8 W

  H 10 W

  I 18 W

Science in Action

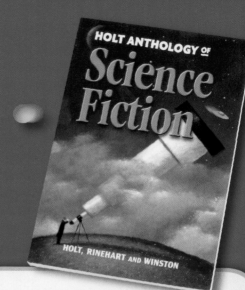

Science, Technology, and Society

Wearable Computers

Today's thin, portable laptop computers are extremely tiny compared to the first general-purpose computer, ENIAC, which filled an entire room. But today's laptops may look bulky next to the computers of tomorrow. In the future, you might wear your computer! A wearable computer is always with you, like clothing or eyeglasses. It is easy to operate. You can even use it while moving around. You might use a wearable computer to take notes in class, look up a phone number, check e-mail, or browse the Internet. These computers are already being used today by a number of companies. As the technology evolves, wearable computers will become even easier to use and more advanced in the types of tasks they perform.

Math ACTIVITY

One wearable computer that is available today can operate from 0°C to 50°C. You can convert temperature measurements from Celsius to Fahrenheit with this equation: Fahrenheit temperature = (9/5 × Celsius temperature) + 32. What is the operating range of this computer in degrees Fahrenheit?

Science Fiction

"There Will Come Soft Rains" by Ray Bradbury

Ticktock, seven o'clock, time to get up, seven o'clock. The voice clock in the living room sent out the wake-up message, gently calling to the family to get up and begin their new day. A few minutes later, the automatic stove in the kitchen began the family breakfast. A soft rain was falling outside, so the weather box by the front door suggested that raincoats were necessary today.

But no family sounds come from the house. The house goes on talking to itself as if it were keeping itself company. Why doesn't anyone answer? Find out when you read Ray Bradbury's "There Will Come Soft Rains" in the *Holt Anthology of Science Fiction*.

Language Arts ACTIVITY

WRITING SKILL The story described above takes place in 2026. The author has imagined how the future world might be. Write a short story about how you think life will be different in the year 2050.

Agnes Riley

Computer Technician Some people take it for granted how smoothly a computer works—until it breaks down. When that happens, you may need to call in an expert, such as Agnes Riley. Agnes is a computer technician from Budapest, Hungary. When a computer isn't working properly, she will take it apart, find the problem, and fix it.

Many people go to school to learn about computer repair, but Agnes taught herself. In Hungary, the company she worked for had a set of old, run-down computers. Agnes started experimenting, trying to repair them. The more she tinkered, the more she learned.

When Agnes moved to New York City in 1999, she wanted to become a computer technician. She started out as a computer salesperson. Eventually, she got the technician training materials. Her earlier experimenting and her studying paid off. She passed the exam to become a licensed technician. Agnes enjoys solving problems and likes helping people. If you are the same type of person, you might want to become a computer technician, too!

Social Studies ACTiViTy

WRITING SKILL Agnes Riley is from Budapest, Hungary. What might you see if you visited Budapest? Do some research to find out, and then design a travel brochure to encourage tourists to visit the city. You might include information about local points of interest or Budapest's history.

To learn more about these Science in Action topics, visit go.hrw.com and type in the keyword HP5ELTF.

Current Science

Check out Current Science® articles related to this chapter by visiting go.hrw.com. Just type in the keyword HP5CS19.

Skills Practice Lab

Stop the Static Electricity!

Imagine this scenario: Some of your clothes cling together when they come out of the dryer. This annoying problem is caused by static electricity—the buildup of electric charges on an object. In this lab, you'll discover how this buildup occurs.

MATERIALS

- cloth, silk
- cloth, woolen
- packing peanut, plastic-foam
- rod, glass
- rod, rubber
- tape
- thread, 30 cm

SAFETY

Ask a Question

1 How do electric charges build up on clothes in a dryer?

Form a Hypothesis

2 Write a statement that answers the question above. Explain your reasoning.

Test the Hypothesis

3 Tie a piece of thread approximately 30 cm in length to a packing peanut. Hang the peanut by the thread from the edge of a table. Tape the thread to the table.

4 Rub the rubber rod with the wool cloth for 10 to 15 s. Bring the rod near, but do not touch, the peanut. Observe the peanut, and record your observations. If nothing happens, repeat this step.

5 Touch the peanut with the rubber rod. Pull the rod away from the peanut, and then bring it near again. Record your observations.

6 Repeat steps 4 and 5 with the glass rod and silk cloth.

7 Now, rub the rubber rod with the wool cloth, and bring the rod near the peanut again. Record your observations.

Analyze the Results

1 What caused the peanut to act differently in steps 4 and 5?

2 Did the glass rod have the same effect on the peanut as the rubber rod did? Explain how the peanut reacted in each case.

3 Was the reaction of the peanut the same in steps 5 and 7? Explain.

Draw Conclusions

4 Based on your results, was your hypothesis correct? Explain your answer, and write a new statement if necessary.

Applying Your Data

Do some research to find out how a dryer sheet helps stop the buildup of electric charges in the dryer.

Model-Making Lab

Potato Power

Have you ever wanted to look inside a D cell from a flashlight or an AA cell from a portable radio? All cells include the same basic components, as shown below. There is a metal "bucket," some electrolyte (a paste), and a rod of some other metal (or solid) in the middle. Even though cell construction is simple, companies that manufacture cells are always trying to make a product with the highest voltage possible from the least expensive materials. Sometimes, companies try different pastes, and sometimes they try different combinations of metals. In this lab, you will make your own cell. Using inexpensive materials, you will try to produce the highest voltage you can.

MATERIALS

- metal strips, labeled
- potato
- ruler, metric
- voltmeter

SAFETY

Procedure

1. Choose two metal strips. Carefully push one of the strips into the potato at least 2 cm deep. Insert the second strip the same way, and measure how far apart the two strips are. (If one of your metal strips is too soft to push into the potato, push a harder strip in first, remove it, and then push the soft strip into the slit.) Record the two metals you have used and the distance between the strips. **Caution:** The strips of metal may have sharp edges.

2. Connect the voltmeter to the two strips, and record the voltage.

3. Move one of the strips closer to or farther from the other. Measure the new distance and voltage. Record your results.

4. Repeat steps 1 through 3, using different combinations of metal strips and distances until you find the combination that produces the highest voltage.

Metal "bucket"

Electrolyte

Metal or carbon rod

D cell

Analyze the Results

1. What combination of metals and distance produced the highest voltage?

2. If you change only the distance but use the same metal strips, what is the effect on the voltage?

3. One of the metal strips tends to lose electrons, and the other tends to gain electrons. What do you think would happen if you used two strips of the same metal?

Skills Practice Lab

Magnetic Mystery

MATERIALS

- acetate, clear (1 sheet)
- iron filings
- magnets, different shapes (2)
- shoe box
- tape, masking

SAFETY

Every magnet is surrounded by a magnetic field. Magnetic field lines show the shape of the magnetic field. These lines can be modeled by using iron filings. The iron filings are affected by the magnetic field, and they fall into lines showing the field. In this lab, you will first learn about magnetic fields, and then you will use this knowledge to identify a mystery magnet's shape and orientation based on observations of the field lines.

Ask a Question

1 Can a magnet's shape and orientation be determined without seeing the magnet?

Form a Hypothesis

2 Write a possible answer to the question above. Explain your reasoning.

Test the Hypothesis

3 Lay one of the magnets flat on a table.

4 Place a sheet of clear acetate over the magnet. Sprinkle some iron filings on the acetate to see the magnetic field lines.

5 Draw the magnet and the magnetic field lines.

6 Remove the acetate, and return the filings to the container.

7 Place your magnet so that one end is pointing up. Repeat steps 4 through 6.

8 Place your magnet on its side. Repeat steps 4 through 6.

9 Repeat steps 3 through 8 with the other magnet.

10 Remove the lid from a shoe box, and tape a magnet underneath the lid. Once the magnet is secure, place the lid on the box.

11 Exchange boxes with another team.

12 Without opening the box, use the sheet of acetate and the iron filings to determine the shape of the magnetic field.

13 Draw the magnetic field lines.

Analyze the Results

1 Use your drawings from steps 3 through 9 to find the shape and orientation of the magnet in your box. Draw a picture of your conclusion.

Applying Your Data

Examine your drawings. Can you identify the north and south poles of a magnet from the shape of the magnetic field lines? Design a procedure that would allow you to determine the poles of a magnet.

Skills Practice Lab

Electricity from Magnetism

You use electricity every day. But did you ever wonder where it comes from? Some of the electrical energy you use is converted from chemical energy in cells or batteries. But where does the electrical energy come from when you plug a lamp into a wall outlet? In this lab, you will see how electricity can be generated from magnetism.

Ask a Question

1 How can electricity be generated from magnetism?

Form a Hypothesis

2 Write a statement to answer question 1.

Test the Hypothesis

3 Sand the enamel off the last 2 cm or 3 cm of each end of the magnet wire. Wrap the magnet wire around the tube to make a coil, as illustrated below. Using the insulated wires, attach the bare ends of the wire to the galvanometer.

4 While watching the galvanometer, move a bar magnet into the coil, hold it there for a moment, and then remove it. Record your observations.

5 Repeat step 4 several times, moving the magnet at different speeds. Observe the galvanometer carefully.

6 Hold the magnet still, and pass the coil over the magnet. Record your observations.

Analyze the Results

1 How does the speed of the magnet affect the size of the electric current?

2 How is the direction of the electric current affected by the motion of the magnet?

3 Examine your hypothesis. Is your hypothesis accurate? Explain. If necessary, write a new hypothesis to answer question 1.

Draw Conclusions

4 Would an electric current still be generated if the wire were broken? Why or why not?

5 Could a stationary magnet be used to generate an electric current? Explain.

6 What energy conversions occur in this investigation?

7 Write a short paragraph that explains the requirements for generating electricity from magnetism.

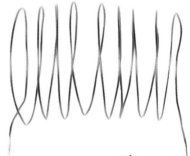

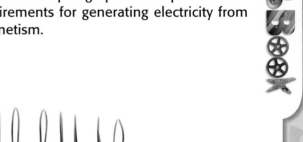

Model-Making Lab

Tune In!

You probably have listened to radios many times in your life. Modern radios are complicated electronic devices. However, radios do not have to be so complicated. The basic parts of all radios include a diode, an inductor, a capacitor, an antenna, a ground wire, and an earphone (or a speaker and amplifier on a large radio). In this activity, you will examine each of these components one at a time as you build a working model of a radio-wave receiver.

Ask a Question

1 Write a question you can test using the procedure in this lab.

Form a Hypothesis

2 Write a possible answer to the question you wrote in the step above. Explain your reasoning.

Test the Hypothesis

3 Examine the diode. Describe it on another sheet of paper.

4 A diode carries current in only one direction. Draw the inside of a diode, and illustrate how the diode might allow current in only one direction.

5 An inductor controls the amount of electric current because of the resistance of the wire. Make an inductor by winding the insulated wire around a cardboard tube approximately 100 times. Wind the wire so that all the turns of the coil are neat and in an orderly row, as shown below. Leave about 25 cm of wire on each end of the coil. The coil of wire may be held on the tube using tape.

MATERIALS

- aluminum foil
- antenna
- cardboard, 20 cm × 30 cm
- cardboard tubes (2)
- connecting wires, 30 cm each (7)
- diode
- earphone
- ground wire
- paper (1 sheet)
- paper clips (3)
- scissors
- tape
- wire, insulated, 2 m

SAFETY

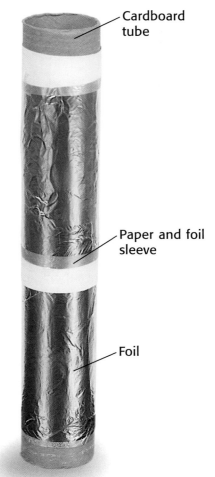

6 Now, you will construct the variable capacitor. A capacitor stores electrical energy when an electric current is applied. A variable capacitor is a capacitor in which the amount of energy stored can be changed. Cut a piece of aluminum foil to go around the tube but only half the length of the tube, as shown at right. Keep the foil as wrinkle-free as possible as you wrap it around the tube, and tape the foil to itself. Now, tape the foil to the tube.

7 Use the sheet of paper and tape to make a sliding cover on the tube. The paper should completely cover the foil on the tube with about 1 cm extra.

8 Cut another sheet of aluminum foil to wrap completely around the paper. Leave approximately 1 cm of paper showing at each end of the foil. Tape this foil sheet to the paper sleeve. If you have done this correctly, you have a paper/foil sheet that will slide up and down the tube over the stationary foil. The two pieces of foil should not touch.

9 Stand your variable capacitor on its end so that the stationary foil is at the bottom. The amount of stored energy is greater when the sleeve is down than when the sleeve is up.

10 Use tape to attach one connecting wire to the stationary foil at the end of the tube. Use tape to attach another connecting wire to the sliding foil sleeve. Be sure that the metal part of the wire touches the foil.

Cardboard tube

Paper and foil sleeve

Foil

Capacitor

Partially Completed Model Receiver

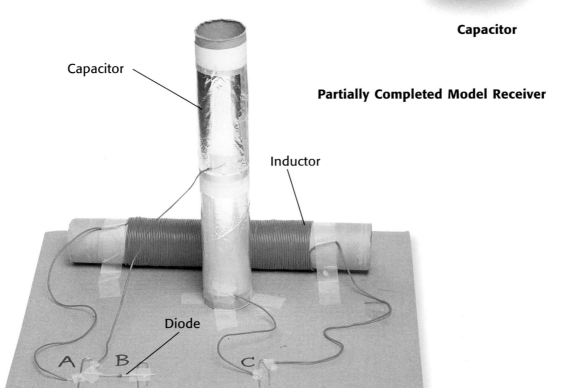

Capacitor

Inductor

Diode

A B C

11 Hook three paper clips on one edge of the cardboard, as shown below. Label one paper clip "A," the second one "B," and the third one "C."

12 Lay the inductor on the piece of cardboard, and tape it to the cardboard.

13 Stand the capacitor next to the inductor, and tape the tube to the cardboard. Be sure not to tape the sleeve—it must be free to slide.

14 Use tape to connect the diode to paper clips A and B. The cathode should be closest to paper clip B. (The cathode end of the diode is the one with the dark band.) Make sure that all connections have good metal-to-metal contact.

15 Connect one end of the inductor to paper clip A and the other end to paper clip C. Use tape to hold the wires in place.

16 Connect the wire from the sliding part of the capacitor to paper clip A. Connect the other wire (from the stationary foil) to paper clip C.

17 The antenna receives radio waves transmitted by a radio station. Tape a connecting wire to your antenna. Then, connect this wire to paper clip A.

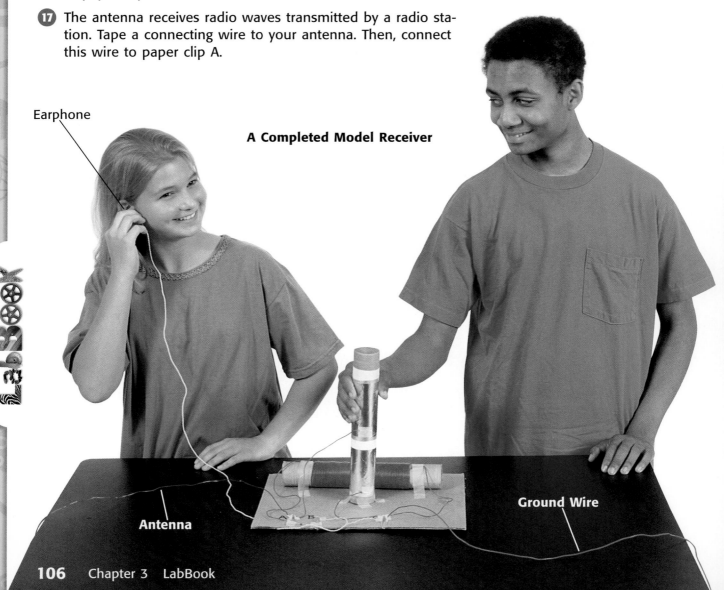

Earphone

A Completed Model Receiver

Antenna

Ground Wire

18 Use tape to connect one end of the ground wire to paper clip C. The other end of the ground wire should be connected to an object specified by your teacher.

19 The earphone will allow you to detect the radio waves you receive. Connect one wire from the earphone to paper clip B and the other wire to paper clip C.

20 You are now ready to begin listening. With everything connected and the earphone in your ear, slowly slide the paper/foil sheet of the capacitor up and down. Listen for a very faint sound. You may have to troubleshoot many of the parts to get your receiver to work. As you troubleshoot, check to be sure there is good contact between all the connections.

Analyze the Results

1 Describe the process of operating your receiver.

2 Considering what you have learned about a diode, why is it important to have the diode connected the correct way?

3 A function of the inductor on a radio is to "slow the current down." Why does the inductor you made slow the current down more than does a straight wire the length of your coil?

4 A capacitor consists of any two conductors separated by an insulator. For your capacitor, list the two conductors and the insulator.

Draw Conclusions

5 Explain why the amount of stored energy is increased down when you slide the foil sleeve and decreased when you slide the foil sleeve up.

6 Make a list of ways that your receiver is similar to a modern radio. Make a second list of ways that your receiver is different from a modern radio.

Contents

Reading Check Answers 109
Study Skills 110
SI Measurement 116
Temperature Scales 117
Measuring Skills 118
Scientific Methods 119
Making Charts and Graphs 121
Math Refresher 124
Physical Science Laws and Principles 128

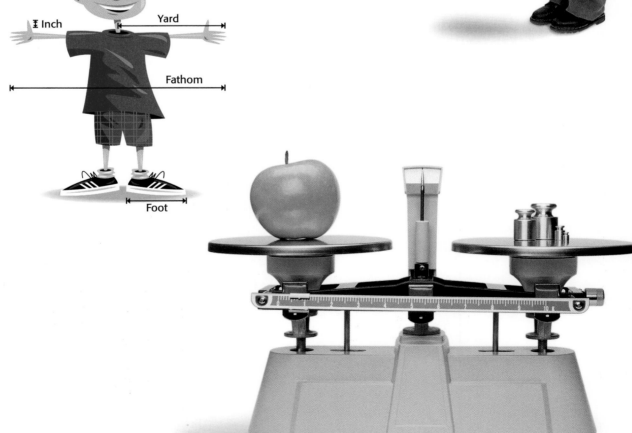

Appendix

✔ *Reading Check* Answers

Chapter 1   Introduction to Electricity

Section 1
Page 4: protons and electrons
Page 6: friction, conduction, and induction
Page 7: You can use an electroscope to detect whether an object is charged.
Page 9: Electric discharge is the release of electricity stored in a source.
Page 10: Sample answer: A person in an open area might be the tallest object and might provide a path for lightning.

Section 2
Page 12: amperes (A)
Page 13: alternating current (AC) and direct current (DC)
Page 14: volts (V)
Page 17: wet cells and dry cells
Page 18: a photocell

Section 3
Page 21: watt (W) and kilowatt (kW)
Page 22: kilowatt-hour (kWh)

Section 4
Page 24: an energy source, wires, and a load
Page 25: series circuits and parallel circuits
Page 26: Loads are connected in a single loop in a series circuit.
Page 27: Loads are connected side by side in branches in a parallel circuit.
Page 28: fuses and circuit breakers

Chapter 2   Electromagnetism

Section 1
Page 40: A magnet is any material that attracts iron or things made of iron.
Page 41: The poles of the magnets are identical.
Page 42: The magnetic fields of the individual atoms cancel each other out.
Page 43: A magnet can lose its magnetic properties if it is dropped, hit, placed in a strong magnetic field that is opposite to its own, or heated.
Page 44: Ferromagnets are magnets made of iron, nickel, cobalt, or mixtures of these metals.
Page 46: Scientists think that the Earth's magnetic field is caused by the movement of electric charges in the Earth's liquid outer core.

Section 2
Page 49: the interaction between electricity and magnetism
Page 50: The magnetic field gets stronger.
Page 51: The electric current creates a magnetic field that exerts a force on the compass needle and causes the compass needle to move.
Page 53: electric current

Section 3
Page 54: Faraday was trying to induce a current in a wire by using the magnetic field of an electromagnet.
Page 56: Mechanical energy is converted into electrical energy in an electric generator.
Page 57: A nuclear reaction, fossil fuels, and wind are sources of energy that are used to generate electrical energy.
Page 58: A transformer increases or decreases the voltage of alternating current.

Chapter 3   Electronic Technology

Section 1
Page 71: The conductivity of the semiconductor is changed by doping.
Page 72: A diode allows current in only one direction, so it blocks current that is in the other direction.
Page 73: NPN and PNP
Page 74: Devices can be made smaller and can run faster by using integrated circuits.

Section 2
Page 77: An analog signal is a signal whose properties can change continuously in a given range.
Page 79: A digital recording can be made to sound more like the original sound by taking more samples each second.
Page 81: analog signals and digital signals
Page 82: A plasma display does not use electron beams to activate the phosphors. Instead, each tiny cell that contains phosphor is activated individually.

Section 3
Page 84: input, processing, storage, and output
Page 85: A microprocessor is a single semiconductor chip that controls and executes a microcomputer's instructions.
Page 86: central processing unit
Page 89: operating-system software and application software
Page 90: Sample answer: The World Wide Web is a collection of pages that share a format that can be viewed on any computer.

Study Skills

FoldNote Instructions

Have you ever tried to study for a test or quiz but didn't know where to start? Or have you read a chapter and found that you can remember only a few ideas? Well, FoldNotes are a fun and exciting way to help you learn and remember the ideas you encounter as you learn science!

FoldNotes are tools that you can use to organize concepts. By focusing on a few main concepts, FoldNotes help you learn and remember how the concepts fit together. They can help you see the "big picture." Below you will find instructions for building 10 different FoldNotes.

Pyramid

1. Place a sheet of paper in front of you. Fold the lower left-hand corner of the paper diagonally to the opposite edge of the paper.

2. Cut off the tab of paper created by the fold (at the top).

3. Open the paper so that it is a square. Fold the lower right-hand corner of the paper diagonally to the opposite corner to form a triangle.

4. Open the paper. The creases of the two folds will have created an X.

5. Using scissors, cut along one of the creases. Start from any corner, and stop at the center point to create two flaps. Use tape or glue to attach one of the flaps on top of the other flap.

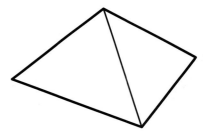

Double Door

1. Fold a sheet of paper in half from the top to the bottom. Then, unfold the paper.

2. Fold the top and bottom edges of the paper to the crease.

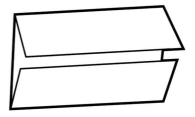

Booklet

1. Fold a sheet of paper in half from left to right. Then, unfold the paper.

2. Fold the sheet of paper in half again from the top to the bottom. Then, unfold the paper.

3. Refold the sheet of paper in half from left to right.

4. Fold the top and bottom edges to the center crease.

5. Completely unfold the paper.

6. Refold the paper from top to bottom.

7. Using scissors, cut a slit along the center crease of the sheet from the folded edge to the creases made in step 4. Do not cut the entire sheet in half.

8. Fold the sheet of paper in half from left to right. While holding the bottom and top edges of the paper, push the bottom and top edges together so that the center collapses at the center slit. Fold the four flaps to form a four-page book.

Layered Book

1. Lay one sheet of paper on top of another sheet. Slide the top sheet up so that 2 cm of the bottom sheet is showing.

2. Hold the two sheets together, fold down the top of the two sheets so that you see four 2 cm tabs along the bottom.

3. Using a stapler, staple the top of the FoldNote.

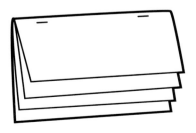

Key-Term Fold

1. Fold a sheet of lined notebook paper in half from left to right.

2. Using scissors, cut along every third line from the right edge of the paper to the center fold to make tabs.

Four-Corner Fold

1. Fold a sheet of paper in half from left to right. Then, unfold the paper.

2. Fold each side of the paper to the crease in the center of the paper.

3. Fold the paper in half from the top to the bottom. Then, unfold the paper.

4. Using scissors, cut the top flap creases made in step 3 to form four flaps.

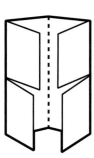

Three-Panel Flip Chart

1. Fold a piece of paper in half from the top to the bottom.

2. Fold the paper in thirds from side to side. Then, unfold the paper so that you can see the three sections.

3. From the top of the paper, cut along each of the vertical fold lines to the fold in the middle of the paper. You will now have three flaps.

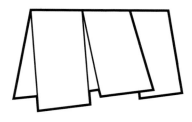

Table Fold

1. Fold a piece of paper in half from the top to the bottom. Then, fold the paper in half again.

2. Fold the paper in thirds from side to side.

3. Unfold the paper completely. Carefully trace the fold lines by using a pen or pencil.

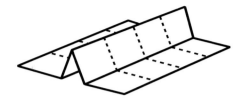

Two-Panel Flip Chart

1. Fold a piece of paper in half from the top to the bottom.

2. Fold the paper in half from side to side. Then, unfold the paper so that you can see the two sections.

3. From the top of the paper, cut along the vertical fold line to the fold in the middle of the paper. You will now have two flaps.

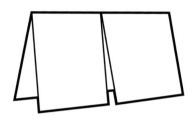

Tri-Fold

1. Fold a piece a paper in thirds from the top to the bottom.

2. Unfold the paper so that you can see the three sections. Then, turn the paper sideways so that the three sections form vertical columns.

3. Trace the fold lines by using a pen or pencil. Label the columns "Know," "Want," and "Learn."

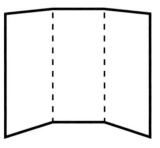

Appendix

Graphic Organizer Instructions

Have you ever wished that you could "draw out" the many concepts you learn in your science class? Sometimes, being able to *see* how concepts are related really helps you remember what you've learned. Graphic Organizers do just that! They give you a way to draw or map out concepts.

All you need to make a Graphic Organizer is a piece of paper and a pencil. Below you will find instructions for four different Graphic Organizers designed to help you organize the concepts you'll learn in this book.

Spider Map

1. Draw a diagram like the one shown. In the circle, write the main topic.

2. From the circle, draw legs to represent different categories of the main topic. You can have as many categories as you want.

3. From the category legs, draw horizontal lines. As you read the chapter, write details about each category on the horizontal lines.

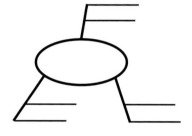

Comparison Table

1. Draw a chart like the one shown. Your chart can have as many columns and rows as you want.

2. In the top row, write the topics that you want to compare.

3. In the left column, write characteristics of the topics that you want to compare. As you read the chapter, fill in the characteristics for each topic in the appropriate boxes.

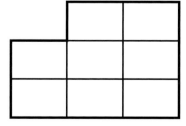

Chain-of-Events-Chart

1. Draw a box. In the box, write the first step of a process or the first event of a timeline.

2. Under the box, draw another box, and use an arrow to connect the two boxes. In the second box, write the next step of the process or the next event in the timeline.

3. Continue adding boxes until the process or timeline is finished.

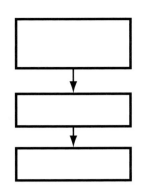

Concept Map

1. Draw a circle in the center of a piece of paper. Write the main idea of the chapter in the center of the circle.

2. From the circle, draw other circles. In those circles, write characteristics of the main idea. Draw arrows from the center circle to the circles that contain the characteristics.

3. From each circle that contains a characteristic, draw other circles. In those circles, write specific details about the characteristic. Draw arrows from each circle that contains a characteristic to the circles that contain specific details. You may draw as many circles as you want.

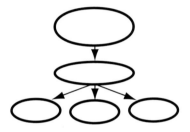

Appendix

SI Measurement

The International System of Units, or SI, is the standard system of measurement used by many scientists. Using the same standards of measurement makes it easier for scientists to communicate with one another.

SI works by combining prefixes and base units. Each base unit can be used with different prefixes to define smaller and larger quantities. The table below lists common SI prefixes.

SI Prefixes

Prefix	Symbol	Factor	Example
kilo-	k	1,000	kilogram, 1 kg = 1,000 g
hecto-	h	100	hectoliter, 1 hL = 100 L
deka-	da	10	dekameter, 1 dam = 10 m
		1	meter, liter, gram
deci-	d	0.1	decigram, 1 dg = 0.1 g
centi-	c	0.01	centimeter, 1 cm = 0.01 m
milli-	m	0.001	milliliter, 1 mL = 0.001 L
micro-	μ	0.000 001	micrometer, 1 μm = 0.000 001 m

SI Conversion Table

SI units	From SI to English	From English to SI
Length		
kilometer (km) = 1,000 m	1 km = 0.621 mi	1 mi = 1.609 km
meter (m) = 100 cm	1 m = 3.281 ft	1 ft = 0.305 m
centimeter (cm) = 0.01 m	1 cm = 0.394 in.	1 in. = 2.540 cm
millimeter (mm) = 0.001 m	1 mm = 0.039 in.	
micrometer (μm) = 0.000 001 m		
nanometer (nm) = 0.000 000 001 m		
Area		
square kilometer (km^2) = 100 hectares	1 km^2 = 0.386 mi^2	1 mi^2 = 2.590 km^2
hectare (ha) = 10,000 m^2	1 ha = 2.471 acres	1 acre = 0.405 ha
square meter (m^2) = 10,000 cm^2	1 m^2 = 10.764 ft^2	1 ft^2 = 0.093 m^2
square centimeter (cm^2) = 100 mm^2	1 cm^2 = 0.155 in.^{2}	1 in.^{2} = 6.452 cm^2
Volume		
liter (L) = 1,000 mL = 1 dm^3	1 L = 1.057 fl qt	1 fl qt = 0.946 L
milliliter (mL) = 0.001 L = 1 cm^3	1 mL = 0.034 fl oz	1 fl oz = 29.574 mL
microliter (μL) = 0.000 001 L		
Mass		
kilogram (kg) = 1,000 g	1 kg = 2.205 lb	1 lb = 0.454 kg
gram (g) = 1,000 mg	1 g = 0.035 oz	1 oz = 28.350 g
milligram (mg) = 0.001 g		
microgram (μg) = 0.000 001 g		

Temperature Scales

Temperature can be expressed by using three different scales: Fahrenheit, Celsius, and Kelvin. The SI unit for temperature is the kelvin (K).

Although 0 K is much colder than 0°C, a change of 1 K is equal to a change of 1°C.

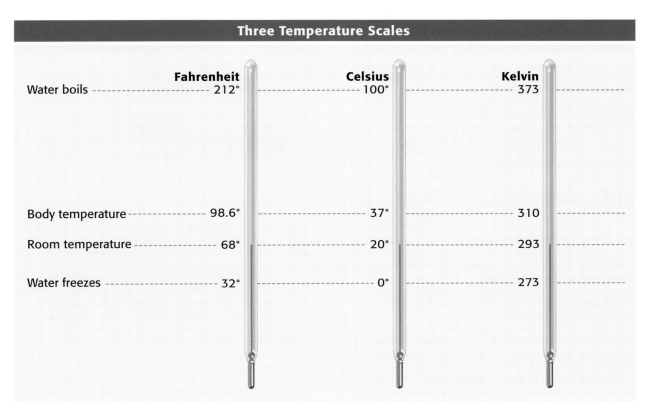

Three Temperature Scales

	Fahrenheit	Celsius	Kelvin
Water boils	212°	100°	373
Body temperature	98.6°	37°	310
Room temperature	68°	20°	293
Water freezes	32°	0°	273

Temperature Conversions Table

To convert	Use this equation:	Example
Celsius to Fahrenheit °C → °F	$°F = \left(\dfrac{9}{5} \times °C\right) + 32$	Convert 45°C to °F. $°F = \left(\dfrac{9}{5} \times 45°C\right) + 32 = 113°F$
Fahrenheit to Celsius °F → °C	$°C = \dfrac{5}{9} \times (°F - 32)$	Convert 68°F to °C. $°C = \dfrac{5}{9} \times (68°F - 32) = 20°C$
Celsius to Kelvin °C → K	$K = °C + 273$	Convert 45°C to K. $K = 45°C + 273 = 318\ K$
Kelvin to Celsius K → °C	$°C = K - 273$	Convert 32 K to °C. $°C = 32K - 273 = -241°C$

Appendix

Measuring Skills

Using a Graduated Cylinder

When using a graduated cylinder to measure volume, keep the following procedures in mind:

1. Place the cylinder on a flat, level surface before measuring liquid.

2. Move your head so that your eye is level with the surface of the liquid.

3. Read the mark closest to the liquid level. On glass graduated cylinders, read the mark closest to the center of the curve in the liquid's surface.

Using a Meterstick or Metric Ruler

When using a meterstick or metric ruler to measure length, keep the following procedures in mind:

1. Place the ruler firmly against the object that you are measuring.

2. Align one edge of the object exactly with the 0 end of the ruler.

3. Look at the other edge of the object to see which of the marks on the ruler is closest to that edge. (Note: Each small slash between the centimeters represents a millimeter, which is one-tenth of a centimeter.)

Using a Triple-Beam Balance

When using a triple-beam balance to measure mass, keep the following procedures in mind:

1. Make sure the balance is on a level surface.

2. Place all of the countermasses at 0. Adjust the balancing knob until the pointer rests at 0.

3. Place the object you wish to measure on the pan. **Caution:** Do not place hot objects or chemicals directly on the balance pan.

4. Move the largest countermass along the beam to the right until it is at the last notch that does not tip the balance. Follow the same procedure with the next-largest countermass. Then, move the smallest countermass until the pointer rests at 0.

5. Add the readings from the three beams together to determine the mass of the object.

6. When determining the mass of crystals or powders, first find the mass of a piece of filter paper. Then, add the crystals or powder to the paper, and remeasure. The actual mass of the crystals or powder is the total mass minus the mass of the paper. When finding the mass of liquids, first find the mass of the empty container. Then, find the combined mass of the liquid and container. The mass of the liquid is the total mass minus the mass of the container.

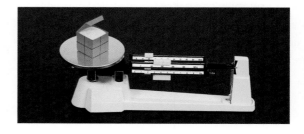

Scientific Methods

The ways in which scientists answer questions and solve problems are called **scientific methods.** The same steps are often used by scientists as they look for answers. However, there is more than one way to use these steps. Scientists may use all of the steps or just some of the steps during an investigation. They may even repeat some of the steps. The goal of using scientific methods is to come up with reliable answers and solutions.

Six Steps of Scientific Methods

 **1 Ask a Question**

Good questions come from careful **observations.** You make observations by using your senses to gather information. Sometimes, you may use instruments, such as microscopes and telescopes, to extend the range of your senses. As you observe the natural world, you will discover that you have many more questions than answers. These questions drive investigations.

Questions beginning with *what, why, how,* and *when* are important in focusing an investigation. Here is an example of a question that could lead to an investigation.

Question: How does acid rain affect plant growth?

 **2 Form a Hypothesis**

After you ask a question, you need to form a **hypothesis.** A hypothesis is a clear statement of what you expect the answer to your question to be. Your hypothesis will represent your best "educated guess" based on what you have observed and what you already know. A good hypothesis is testable. Otherwise, the investigation can go no further. Here is a hypothesis based on the question, "How does acid rain affect plant growth?"

Hypothesis: Acid rain slows plant growth.

The hypothesis can lead to predictions. A prediction is what you think the outcome of your experiment or data collection will be. Predictions are usually stated in an if-then format. Here is a sample prediction for the hypothesis that acid rain slows plant growth.

Prediction: If a plant is watered with only acid rain (which has a pH of 4), then the plant will grow at half its normal rate.

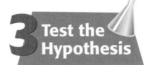 **3 Test the Hypothesis**

After you have formed a hypothesis and made a prediction, your hypothesis should be tested. One way to test a hypothesis is with a controlled experiment. A **controlled experiment** tests only one factor at a time. In an experiment to test the effect of acid rain on plant growth, the **control group** would be watered with normal rain water. The **experimental group** would be watered with acid rain. All of the plants should receive the same amount of sunlight and water each day. The air temperature should be the same for all groups. However, the acidity of the water will be a variable. In fact, any factor that is different from one group to another is a **variable.** If your hypothesis is correct, then the acidity of the water and plant growth are *dependant variables.* The amount a plant grows is dependent on the acidity of the water. However, the amount of water each plant receives and the amount of sunlight each plant receives are *independent variables.* Either of these factors could change without affecting the other factor.

Sometimes, the nature of an investigation makes a controlled experiment impossible. For example, the Earth's core is surrounded by thousands of meters of rock. Under such circumstances, a hypothesis may be tested by making detailed observations.

 **4 Analyze the Results**

After you have completed your experiments, made your observations, and collected your data, you must analyze all the information you have gathered. Tables and graphs are often used in this step to organize the data.

5 Draw Conclusions

After analyzing your data, you can determine if your results support your hypothesis. If your hypothesis is supported, you (or others) might want to repeat the observations or experiments to verify your results. If your hypothesis is not supported by the data, you may have to check your procedure for errors. You may even have to reject your hypothesis and make a new one. If you cannot draw a conclusion from your results, you may have to try the investigation again or carry out further observations or experiments.

6 Communicate Results

After any scientific investigation, you should report your results. By preparing a written or oral report, you let others know what you have learned. They may repeat your investigation to see if they get the same results. Your report may even lead to another question and then to another investigation.

Scientific Methods in Action

Scientific methods contain loops in which several steps may be repeated over and over again. In some cases, certain steps are unnecessary. Thus, there is not a "straight line" of steps. For example, sometimes scientists find that testing one hypothesis raises new questions and new hypotheses to be tested. And sometimes, testing the hypothesis leads directly to a conclusion. Furthermore, the steps in scientific methods are not always used in the same order. Follow the steps in the diagram, and see how many different directions scientific methods can take you.

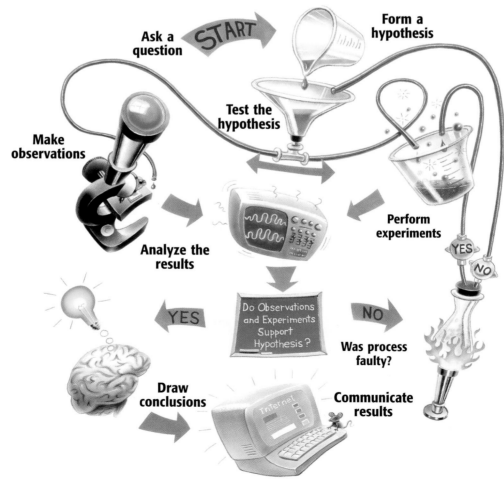

Making Charts and Graphs

Pie Charts

A pie chart shows how each group of data relates to all of the data. Each part of the circle forming the chart represents a category of the data. The entire circle represents all of the data. For example, a biologist studying a hardwood forest in Wisconsin found that there were five different types of trees. The data table at right summarizes the biologist's findings.

Wisconsin Hardwood Trees	
Type of tree	Number found
Oak	600
Maple	750
Beech	300
Birch	1,200
Hickory	150
Total	3,000

How to Make a Pie Chart

1 To make a pie chart of these data, first find the percentage of each type of tree. Divide the number of trees of each type by the total number of trees, and multiply by 100.

$$\frac{600 \text{ oak}}{3,000 \text{ trees}} \times 100 = 20\%$$

$$\frac{750 \text{ maple}}{3,000 \text{ trees}} \times 100 = 25\%$$

$$\frac{300 \text{ beech}}{3,000 \text{ trees}} \times 100 = 10\%$$

$$\frac{1,200 \text{ birch}}{3,000 \text{ trees}} \times 100 = 40\%$$

$$\frac{150 \text{ hickory}}{3,000 \text{ trees}} \times 100 = 5\%$$

2 Now, determine the size of the wedges that make up the pie chart. Multiply each percentage by 360°. Remember that a circle contains 360°.

$20\% \times 360° = 72°$ $\quad$ $25\% \times 360° = 90°$

$10\% \times 360° = 36°$ $\quad$ $40\% \times 360° = 144°$

$5\% \times 360° = 18°$

3 Check that the sum of the percentages is 100 and the sum of the degrees is 360.

$20\% + 25\% + 10\% + 40\% + 5\% = 100\%$

$72° + 90° + 36° + 144° + 18° = 360°$

4 Use a compass to draw a circle and mark the center of the circle.

5 Then, use a protractor to draw angles of 72°, 90°, 36°, 144°, and 18° in the circle.

6 Finally, label each part of the chart, and choose an appropriate title.

A Community of Wisconsin Hardwood Trees

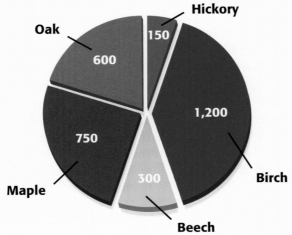

Line Graphs

Line graphs are most often used to demonstrate continuous change. For example, Mr. Smith's students analyzed the population records for their hometown, Appleton, between 1900 and 2000. Examine the data at right.

Because the year and the population change, they are the *variables*. The population is determined by, or dependent on, the year. Therefore, the population is called the **dependent variable,** and the year is called the **independent variable.** Each set of data is called a **data pair.** To prepare a line graph, you must first organize data pairs into a table like the one at right.

Population of Appleton, 1900–2000	
Year	**Population**
1900	1,800
1920	2,500
1940	3,200
1960	3,900
1980	4,600
2000	5,300

How to Make a Line Graph

1 Place the independent variable along the horizontal (*x*) axis. Place the dependent variable along the vertical (*y*) axis.

2 Label the *x*-axis "Year" and the *y*-axis "Population." Look at your largest and smallest values for the population. For the *y*-axis, determine a scale that will provide enough space to show these values. You must use the same scale for the entire length of the axis. Next, find an appropriate scale for the *x*-axis.

3 Choose reasonable starting points for each axis.

4 Plot the data pairs as accurately as possible.

5 Choose a title that accurately represents the data.

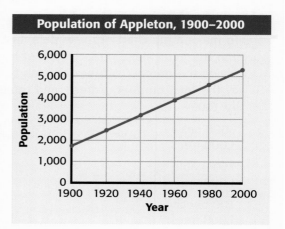

Population of Appleton, 1900–2000

How to Determine Slope

Slope is the ratio of the change in the *y*-value to the change in the *x*-value, or "rise over run."

1 Choose two points on the line graph. For example, the population of Appleton in 2000 was 5,300 people. Therefore, you can define point *a* as (2000, 5,300). In 1900, the population was 1,800 people. You can define point *b* as (1900, 1,800).

2 Find the change in the *y*-value. (*y* at point *a*) − (*y* at point *b*) = 5,300 people − 1,800 people = 3,500 people

3 Find the change in the *x*-value. (*x* at point *a*) − (*x* at point *b*) = 2000 − 1900 = 100 years

4 Calculate the slope of the graph by dividing the change in *y* by the change in *x*.

$$slope = \frac{change\ in\ y}{change\ in\ x}$$

$$slope = \frac{3,500\ people}{100\ years}$$

$$slope = 35\ people\ per\ year$$

In this example, the population in Appleton increased by a fixed amount each year. The graph of these data is a straight line. Therefore, the relationship is **linear.** When the graph of a set of data is not a straight line, the relationship is **nonlinear.**

Using Algebra to Determine Slope

The equation in step 4 may also be arranged to be

$$y = kx$$

where y represents the change in the y-value, k represents the slope, and x represents the change in the x-value.

$$slope = \frac{change\ in\ y}{change\ in\ x}$$

$$k = \frac{y}{x}$$

$$k \times x = \frac{y \times x}{x}$$

$$kx = y$$

Bar Graphs

Bar graphs are used to demonstrate change that is not continuous. These graphs can be used to indicate trends when the data cover a long period of time. A meteorologist gathered the precipitation data shown here for Hartford, Connecticut, for April 1–15, 1996, and used a bar graph to represent the data.

Precipitation in Hartford, Connecticut April 1–15, 1996			
Date	Precipitation (cm)	Date	Precipitation (cm)
April 1	0.5	April 9	0.25
April 2	1.25	April 10	0.0
April 3	0.0	April 11	1.0
April 4	0.0	April 12	0.0
April 5	0.0	April 13	0.25
April 6	0.0	April 14	0.0
April 7	0.0	April 15	6.50
April 8	1.75		

How to Make a Bar Graph

1 Use an appropriate scale and a reasonable starting point for each axis.

2 Label the axes, and plot the data.

3 Choose a title that accurately represents the data.

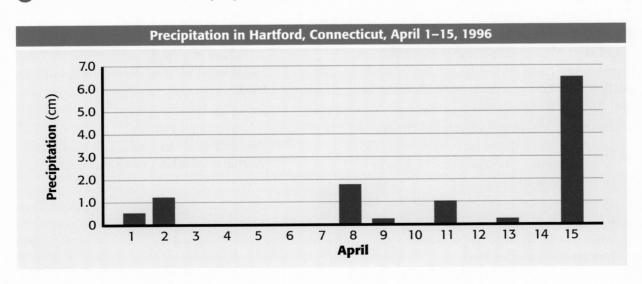

Precipitation in Hartford, Connecticut, April 1–15, 1996

Math Refresher

Science requires an understanding of many math concepts. The following pages will help you review some important math skills.

Averages

An **average,** or **mean,** simplifies a set of numbers into a single number that *approximates* the value of the set.

> **Example:** Find the average of the following set of numbers: 5, 4, 7, and 8.

Step 1: Find the sum.
$$5 + 4 + 7 + 8 = 24$$

Step 2: Divide the sum by the number of numbers in your set. Because there are four numbers in this example, divide the sum by 4.

$$\frac{24}{4} = 6$$

The average, or mean, is **6.**

Ratios

A **ratio** is a comparison between numbers, and it is usually written as a fraction.

> **Example:** Find the ratio of thermometers to students if you have 36 thermometers and 48 students in your class.

Step 1: Make the ratio.
$$\frac{36 \text{ thermometers}}{48 \text{ students}}$$

Step 2: Reduce the fraction to its simplest form.

$$\frac{36}{48} = \frac{36 \div 12}{48 \div 12} = \frac{3}{4}$$

The ratio of thermometers to students is **3 to 4,** or $\frac{3}{4}$. The ratio may also be written in the form 3:4.

Proportions

A **proportion** is an equation that states that two ratios are equal.

$$\frac{3}{1} = \frac{12}{4}$$

To solve a proportion, first multiply across the equal sign. This is called *cross-multiplication.* If you know three of the quantities in a proportion, you can use cross-multiplication to find the fourth.

> **Example:** Imagine that you are making a scale model of the solar system for your science project. The diameter of Jupiter is 11.2 times the diameter of the Earth. If you are using a plastic-foam ball that has a diameter of 2 cm to represent the Earth, what must the diameter of the ball representing Jupiter be?
>
> $$\frac{11.2}{1} = \frac{x}{2 \text{ cm}}$$

Step 1: Cross-multiply.

$$\frac{11.2}{1} \diagup\!\!\!\!\diagdown \frac{x}{2}$$

$$11.2 \times 2 = x \times 1$$

Step 2: Multiply.
$$22.4 = x \times 1$$

Step 3: Isolate the variable by dividing both sides by 1.

$$x = \frac{22.4}{1}$$
$$x = 22.4 \text{ cm}$$

You will need to use a ball that has a diameter of **22.4** cm to represent Jupiter.

Percentages

A **percentage** is a ratio of a given number to 100.

> **Example:** What is 85% of 40?

Step 1: Rewrite the percentage by moving the decimal point two places to the left.

0.85

Step 2: Multiply the decimal by the number that you are calculating the percentage of.

0.85 × 40 = 34

85% of 40 is **34.**

Decimals

To **add** or **subtract decimals,** line up the digits vertically so that the decimal points line up. Then, add or subtract the columns from right to left. Carry or borrow numbers as necessary.

> **Example:** Add the following numbers: 3.1415 and 2.96.

Step 1: Line up the digits vertically so that the decimal points line up.

$$\begin{array}{r} 3.1415 \\ + 2.96 \\ \hline \end{array}$$

Step 2: Add the columns from right to left, and carry when necessary.

$$\begin{array}{r} {}^{1\ 1} \\ 3.1415 \\ + 2.96 \\ \hline 6.1015 \end{array}$$

The sum is **6.1015.**

Fractions

Numbers tell you how many; **fractions** tell you *how much of a whole*.

> **Example:** Your class has 24 plants. Your teacher instructs you to put 5 plants in a shady spot. What fraction of the plants in your class will you put in a shady spot?

Step 1: In the denominator, write the total number of parts in the whole.

$$\frac{?}{24}$$

Step 2: In the numerator, write the number of parts of the whole that are being considered.

$$\frac{5}{24}$$

So, $\frac{5}{24}$ of the plants will be in the shade.

Reducing Fractions

It is usually best to express a fraction in its simplest form. Expressing a fraction in its simplest form is called *reducing* a fraction.

> **Example:** Reduce the fraction $\frac{30}{45}$ to its simplest form.

Step 1: Find the largest whole number that will divide evenly into both the numerator and denominator. This number is called the *greatest common factor* (GCF).

Factors of the numerator 30:

1, 2, 3, 5, 6, 10, **15,** 30

Factors of the denominator 45:

1, 3, 5, 9, **15,** 45

Step 2: Divide both the numerator and the denominator by the GCF, which in this case is 15.

$$\frac{30}{45} = \frac{30 \div 15}{45 \div 15} = \frac{2}{3}$$

Thus, $\frac{30}{45}$ reduced to its simplest form is $\frac{2}{3}$.

Adding and Subtracting Fractions

To **add** or **subtract fractions** that have the **same denominator,** simply add or subtract the numerators.

Examples:

$$\frac{3}{5} + \frac{1}{5} = ? \quad \text{and} \quad \frac{3}{4} - \frac{1}{4} = ?$$

Step 1: Add or subtract the numerators.

$$\frac{3}{5} + \frac{1}{5} = \frac{4}{} \quad \text{and} \quad \frac{3}{4} - \frac{1}{4} = \frac{2}{}$$

Step 2: Write the sum or difference over the denominator.

$$\frac{3}{5} + \frac{1}{5} = \frac{4}{5} \quad \text{and} \quad \frac{3}{4} - \frac{1}{4} = \frac{2}{4}$$

Step 3: If necessary, reduce the fraction to its simplest form.

$\frac{4}{5}$ cannot be reduced, and $\frac{2}{4} = \frac{1}{2}$.

To **add** or **subtract fractions** that have **different denominators,** first find the least common denominator (LCD).

Examples:

$$\frac{1}{2} + \frac{1}{6} = ? \quad \text{and} \quad \frac{3}{4} - \frac{2}{3} = ?$$

Step 1: Write the equivalent fractions that have a common denominator.

$$\frac{3}{6} + \frac{1}{6} = ? \quad \text{and} \quad \frac{9}{12} - \frac{8}{12} = ?$$

Step 2: Add or subtract the fractions.

$$\frac{3}{6} + \frac{1}{6} = \frac{4}{6} \quad \text{and} \quad \frac{9}{12} - \frac{8}{12} = \frac{1}{12}$$

Step 3: If necessary, reduce the fraction to its simplest form.

The fraction $\frac{4}{6} = \frac{2}{3}$, and $\frac{1}{12}$ cannot be reduced.

Multiplying Fractions

To **multiply fractions,** multiply the numerators and the denominators together, and then reduce the fraction to its simplest form.

Example:

$$\frac{5}{9} \times \frac{7}{10} = ?$$

Step 1: Multiply the numerators and denominators.

$$\frac{5}{9} \times \frac{7}{10} = \frac{5 \times 7}{9 \times 10} = \frac{35}{90}$$

Step 2: Reduce the fraction.

$$\frac{35}{90} = \frac{35 \div 5}{90 \div 5} = \frac{7}{18}$$

Dividing Fractions

To **divide fractions,** first rewrite the divisor (the number you divide by) upside down. This number is called the *reciprocal* of the divisor. Then multiply and reduce if necessary.

Example:

$$\frac{5}{8} \div \frac{3}{2} = ?$$

Step 1: Rewrite the divisor as its reciprocal.

$$\frac{3}{2} \rightarrow \frac{2}{3}$$

Step 2: Multiply the fractions.

$$\frac{5}{8} \times \frac{2}{3} = \frac{5 \times 2}{8 \times 3} = \frac{10}{24}$$

Step 3: Reduce the fraction.

$$\frac{10}{24} = \frac{10 \div 2}{24 \div 2} = \frac{5}{12}$$

Appendix

Scientific Notation

Scientific notation is a short way of representing very large and very small numbers without writing all of the place-holding zeros.

> **Example:** Write 653,000,000 in scientific notation.

Step 1: Write the number without the place-holding zeros.

653

Step 2: Place the decimal point after the first digit.

6.53

Step 3: Find the exponent by counting the number of places that you moved the decimal point.

6.53000000

The decimal point was moved eight places to the left. Therefore, the exponent of 10 is positive 8. If you had moved the decimal point to the right, the exponent would be negative.

Step 4: Write the number in scientific notation.

6.53×10^8

Area

Area is the number of square units needed to cover the surface of an object.

> **Formulas:**
>
> $area\ of\ a\ square = side \times side$
> $area\ of\ a\ rectangle = length \times width$
> $area\ of\ a\ triangle = \frac{1}{2} \times base \times height$
>
> **Examples:** Find the areas.

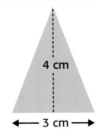

Triangle

$area = \frac{1}{2} \times base \times height$

$area = \frac{1}{2} \times 3\ cm \times 4\ cm$

$area = \textbf{6 cm}^2$

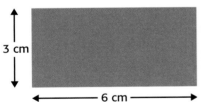

Rectangle

$area = length \times width$

$area = 6\ cm \times 3\ cm$

$area = \textbf{18 cm}^2$

Square

$area = side \times side$

$area = 3\ cm \times 3\ cm$

$area = \textbf{9 cm}^2$

Volume

Volume is the amount of space that something occupies.

> **Formulas:**
>
> $volume\ of\ a\ cube = side \times side \times side$
>
> $volume\ of\ a\ prism = area\ of\ base \times height$
>
> **Examples:**
>
> Find the volume of the solids.

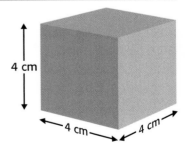

Cube

$volume = side \times side \times side$

$volume = 4\ cm \times 4\ cm \times 4\ cm$

$volume = \textbf{64 cm}^3$

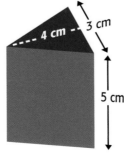

Prism

$volume = area\ of\ base \times height$

$volume = (area\ of\ triangle) \times height$

$volume = (\frac{1}{2} \times 3\ cm \times 4\ cm) \times 5\ cm$

$volume = 6\ cm^2 \times 5\ cm$

$volume = \textbf{30 cm}^3$

Physical Science Laws and Principles

Law of Conservation of Energy

The law of conservation of energy states that energy can be neither created nor destroyed.

The total amount of energy in a closed system is always the same. Energy can be changed from one form to another, but all of the different forms of energy in a system always add up to the same total amount of energy no matter how many energy conversions occur.

Law of Universal Gravitation

The law of universal gravitation states that all objects in the universe attract each other by a force called *gravity*. The size of the force depends on the masses of the objects and the distance between objects.

The first part of the law explains why a bowling ball is much harder to lift than a table-tennis ball. Because the bowling ball has a much larger mass than the table-tennis ball does, the amount of gravity between the Earth and the bowling ball is greater than the amount of gravity between the Earth and the table-tennis ball.

The second part of the law explains why a satellite can remain in orbit around the Earth. The satellite is carefully placed at a distance great enough to prevent the Earth's gravity from immediately pulling the satellite down but small enough to prevent the satellite from completely escaping the Earth's gravity and wandering off into space.

Newton's Laws of Motion

Newton's first law of motion states that an object at rest remains at rest and an object in motion remains in motion at constant speed and in a straight line unless acted on by an unbalanced force.

The first part of the law explains why a football will remain on a tee until it is kicked off or until a gust of wind blows it off.

The second part of the law explains why a bike rider will continue moving forward after the bike comes to an abrupt stop. Gravity and the friction of the sidewalk will eventually stop the rider.

Newton's second law of motion states that the acceleration of an object depends on the mass of the object and the amount of force applied.

The first part of the law explains why the acceleration of a 4 kg bowling ball will be greater than the acceleration of a 6 kg bowling ball if the same force is applied to both.

The second part of the law explains why the acceleration of a bowling ball will be larger if a larger force is applied to the bowling ball.

The relationship of acceleration (*a*) to mass (*m*) and force (*F*) can be expressed mathematically by the following equation:

$$acceleration = \frac{force}{mass}, \text{ or } a = \frac{F}{m}$$

This equation is often rearranged to the form

$$force = mass \times acceleration$$
$$\text{or}$$
$$F = m \times a$$

Newton's third law of motion states that whenever one object exerts a force on a second object, the second object exerts an equal and opposite force on the first.

This law explains that a runner is able to move forward because of the equal and opposite force that the ground exerts on the runner's foot after each step.

Law of Reflection

The law of reflection states that the angle of incidence is equal to the angle of reflection. This law explains why light reflects off a surface at the same angle that the light strikes the surface.

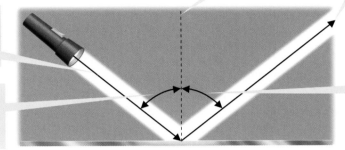

A line perpendicular to the mirror's surface is called the *normal.*

The beam of light reflected off the mirror is called the *reflected beam.*

The beam of light traveling toward the mirror is called the *incident beam.*

The angle between the incident beam and the normal is called the *angle of incidence.*

The angle between the reflected beam and the normal is called the *angle of reflection.*

Charles's Law

Charles's law states that for a fixed amount of gas at a constant pressure, the volume of the gas increases as the temperature of the gas increases. Likewise, the volume of the gas decreases as the temperature of the gas decreases.

If a basketball that was inflated indoors is left outside on a cold winter day, the air particles inside the ball will move more slowly. They will hit the sides of the basketball less often and with less force. The ball will get smaller as the volume of the air decreases.

Boyle's Law

Boyle's law states that for a fixed amount of gas at a constant temperature, the volume of a gas increases as the pressure of the gas decreases. Likewise, the volume of a gas decreases as its pressure increases.

If an inflated balloon is pulled down to the bottom of a swimming pool, the pressure of the water on the balloon increases. The pressure of the air particles inside the balloon must increase to match that of the water outside, so the volume of the air inside the balloon decreases.

Pascal's Principle

Pascal's principle states that a change in pressure at any point in an enclosed fluid will be transmitted equally to all parts of that fluid.

When a mechanic uses a hydraulic jack to raise an automobile off the ground, he or she increases the pressure on the fluid in the jack by pushing on the jack handle. The pressure is transmitted equally to all parts of the fluid-filled jacking system. As fluid presses the jack plate against the frame of the car, the car is lifed off the ground.

Archimedes' Principle

Archimedes' principle states that the buoyant force on an object in a fluid is equal to the weight of the volume of fluid that the object displaces.

A person floating in a swimming pool displaces 20 L of water. The weight of that volume of water is about 200 N. Therefore, the buoyant force on the person is 200 N.

Bernoulli's Principle

Bernoulli's principle states that as the speed of a moving fluid increases, the fluid's pressure decreases.

The lift on an airplane wing or on a Frisbee® can be explained in part by using Bernoulli's principle. Because of the shape of the Frisbee, the air moving over the top of the Frisbee must travel farther than the air below the Frisbee in the same amount of time. In other words, the air above the Frisbee is moving faster than the air below it. This faster-moving air above the Frisbee exerts less pressure than the slower-moving air below it does. The resulting increased pressure below exerts an upward force and pushes the Frisbee up.

Useful Equations

Average speed

$$\text{average speed} = \frac{\text{total distance}}{\text{total time}}$$

Example: A bicycle messenger traveled a distance of 136 km in 8 h. What was the messenger's average speed?

$$\frac{136 \text{ km}}{8 \text{ h}} = 17 \text{ km/h}$$

The messenger's average speed was **17 km/h.**

Average acceleration

$$\frac{\text{average}}{\text{acceleration}} = \frac{\text{final velocity} - \text{starting velocity}}{\text{time it takes to change velocity}}$$

Example: Calculate the average acceleration of an Olympic 100 m dash sprinter who reaches a velocity of 20 m/s south at the finish line. The race was in a straight line and lasted 10 s.

$$\frac{20 \text{ m/s} - 0 \text{ m/s}}{10 \text{s}} = 2 \text{ m/s/s}$$

The sprinter's average acceleration is **2 m/s/s south.**

Net force

Forces in the Same Direction
When forces are in the same direction, add the forces together to determine the net force.

Example: Calculate the net force on a stalled car that is being pushed by two people. One person is pushing with a force of 13 N northwest, and the other person is pushing with a force of 8 N in the same direction.

$$13 \text{ N} + 8 \text{ N} = 21 \text{ N}$$

The net force is **21 N northwest.**

Forces in Opposite Directions
When forces are in opposite directions, subtract the smaller force from the larger force to determine the net force. The net force will be in the direction of the larger force.

Example: Calculate the net force on a rope that is being pulled on each end. One person is pulling on one end of the rope with a force of 12 N south. Another person is pulling on the opposite end of the rope with a force of 7 N north.

$$12 \text{ N} - 7 \text{ N} = 5 \text{ N}$$

The net force is **5 N south.**

Work

Work is done by exerting a force through a distance. Work has units of joules (J), which are equivalent to Newton-meters.

$$Work = F \times d$$

Example: Calculate the amount of work done by a man who lifts a 100 N toddler 1.5 m off the floor.

$Work = 100 \text{ N} \times 1.5 \text{ m} = 150 \text{ N} \bullet \text{m} = 150 \text{ J}$

The man did **150 J** of work.

Power

Power is the rate at which work is done. Power is measured in watts (W), which are equivalent to joules per second.

$$P = \frac{Work}{t}$$

Example: Calculate the power of a weight-lifter who raises a 300 N barbell 2.1 m off the floor in 1.25 s.

$Work = 300 \text{ N} \times 2.1 \text{ m} = 630 \text{ N} \bullet \text{m} = 630 \text{ J}$

$$P = \frac{630 \text{ J}}{1.25 \text{ s}} = \frac{504 \text{ J}}{\text{s}} = 504 \text{ W}$$

The weightlifter has **504 W** of power.

Pressure

Pressure is the force exerted over a given area. The SI unit for pressure is the pascal (Pa).

$$pressure = \frac{force}{area}$$

Example: Calculate the pressure of the air in a soccer ball if the air exerts a force of 25,000 N over an area of 0.15 m^2.

$$pressure = \frac{25,000 \text{ N}}{0.15 \text{ m}^2} = \frac{167,000 \text{ N}}{\text{m}^2} = 167,000 \text{ Pa}$$

The pressure of the air inside the soccer ball is **167,000 Pa.**

Density

$$density = \frac{mass}{volume}$$

Example: Calculate the density of a sponge that has a mass of 10 g and a volume of 40 cm^3.

$$\frac{10 \text{ g}}{40 \text{ cm}^3} = \frac{0.25 \text{ g}}{\text{cm}^3}$$

The density of the sponge is $\frac{0.25 \text{ g}}{\text{cm}^3}$.

Concentration

$$concentration = \frac{mass \ of \ solute}{volume \ of \ solvent}$$

Example: Calculate the concentration of a solution in which 10 g of sugar is dissolved in 125 mL of water.

$$\frac{10 \text{ g of sugar}}{125 \text{ mL of water}} = \frac{0.08 \text{ g}}{\text{mL}}$$

The concentration of this solution is $\frac{0.08 \text{ g}}{\text{mL}}$.

Glossary

A

analog signal (AN uh LAWG SIG nuhl) a signal whose properties can change continuously in a given range (77)

C

cell in electricity, a device that produces an electric current by converting chemical or radiant energy into electrical energy (17)

circuit board a sheet of insulating material that carries circuit elements and that is inserted in an electronic device (70)

computer an electronic device that can accept data and instructions, follow the instructions, and output the results (84)

D

digital signal a signal that can be represented as a sequence of discrete values (78)

diode an electronic device that allows electric charge to move more easily in one direction than in the other (72)

doping (DOHP eeng) the addition of an impurity element to a semiconductor (71)

E

electrical conductor a material in which charges can move freely (8)

electrical insulator a material in which charges cannot move freely (8)

electric current the rate at which charges pass through a given point; measured in amperes (12)

electric discharge the release of electricity stored in a source (9)

electric field the space around a charged object that causes another charged object to experience an electric force (5)

electric force the force of attraction or repulsion on a charged particle that is due to an electric field (5)

electric generator a device that converts mechanical energy into electrical energy (56)

electric motor a device that converts electrical energy into mechanical energy (52)

electric power the rate at which electrical energy is converted into other forms of energy (21)

electromagnet a coil that has a soft iron core and that acts as a magnet when an electric current is in the coil (50)

electromagnetic induction the process of creating a current in a circuit by changing a magnetic field (55)

electromagnetism the interaction between electricity and magnetism (49)

H

hardware the parts or pieces of equipment that make up a computer (86)

I

integrated circuit (IN tuh GRAYT id SUHR kit) a circuit whose components are formed on a single semiconductor (74)

Internet a large computer network that connects many local and smaller networks all over the world (90)

L

law of electric charges the law that states that like charges repel and opposite charges attract (4)

M

magnet any material that attracts iron or materials containing iron (40)

magnetic force the force of attraction or repulsion generated by moving or spinning electric charges (41)

magnetic pole one of two points, such as the ends of a magnet, that have opposing magnetic qualities (40)

microprocessor a single semiconductor chip that controls and executes a microcomputer's instructions (85)

P

parallel circuit a circuit in which the parts are joined in branches such that the potential difference across each part is the same (27)

photocell a device that converts light energy into electrical energy (18)

R

resistance in physical science, the opposition presented to the current by a material or device (15)

S

semiconductor (SEM i kuhn DUHK tuhr) an element or compound that conducts electric current better than an insulator does but not as well as a conductor does (71)

series circuit a circuit in which the parts are joined one after another such that the current in each part is the same (26)

software a set of instructions or commands that tells a computer what to do; a computer program (89)

solenoid a coil of wire with an electric current in it (49)

static electricity electric charge at rest; generally produced by friction or induction (8)

T

thermocouple a device that converts thermal energy into electrical energy (18)

transformer a device that increases or decreases the voltage of alternating current (58)

V

voltage the potential difference between two points; measured in volts (14)

Spanish Glossary

A

analog signal/señal análoga una señal cuyas propiedades cambian continuamente en un rango determinado (77)

C

cell/celda en electricidad, un aparato que produce una corriente eléctrica transformando la energía química o radiante en energía eléctrica (17)

circuit board/cuadro del circuito una lámina de material aislante que lleva elementos del circuito y que es insertado en un aparato electrónico (70)

computer/computadora un aparato electrónico que acepta información e instrucciones, sigue instrucciones y produce una salida para los resultados (84)

D

digital signal/señal digital una señal que se puede representar como una secuencia de valores discretos (78)

diode/diodo un aparato electrónico que permite que la corriente eléctrica pase más fácilmente en una dirección que en otra (72)

doping/adulteración la adición de un elemento impuro a un semiconductor (71)

E

electrical conductor/conductor eléctrico un material en el que las cargas se mueven libremente (8)

electrical insulator/aislante eléctrico un material en el que las cargas no pueden moverse libremente (8)

electric current/corriente eléctrica la tasa a la que las cargas pasan por un punto determinado; se mide en amperes (12)

electric discharge/potencial eléctrico la energía potencial eléctrica asociada con una partícula con carga en relación con la superficie de la Tierra, que tiene un potencial de cero (9)

electric field/carga eléctrica el espacio alrededor de un objeto cargado que hace que otro objeto cargado experimente una fuerza eléctrica (5)

electric force/circuito eléctrico un conjunto de componentes eléctricos conectados de modo que proporcionen una o más rutas completas para el movimiento de las cargas (5)

Electric generator

electric generator/descarga eléctrica la liberación de electricidad almacenada en una fuente (56)

electric motor/campo eléctrico una región en el espacio alrededor de un objeto con carga que hace que un objeto estacionario con carga experimente una fuerza eléctrica (52)

electric power/potencia eléctrica la tasa a la que la energía eléctrica se transforma en otras formas de energía (21)

electromagnet/electroimán una bobina que tiene un centro de hierro suave y que funciona como un imán cuando hay una corriente eléctrica en la bobina (50)

electromagnetic induction/inducción electromagnética el proceso de crear una corriente en un circuito por medio de un cambio en el campo magnético (55)

electromagnetism/electromagnetismo la interacción entre la electricidad y el magnetismo (49)

H

hardware/hardware las partes o piezas de equipo que forman una computadora (86)

I

integrated circuit/circuito integrado un circuito cuyos componentes están formados en un solo semiconductor (74)

Internet/Internet una amplia red de computadoras que conecta muchas redes locales y redes más pequeñas por todo el mundo (90)

L

law of electric charges/ley de las cargas eléctricas la ley que establece que las cargas iguales se repelen y las cargas opuestas se atraen (4)

M

magnet/imán cualquier material que atrae hierro o materiales que contienen hierro (40)

magnetic force/fuerza magnética la fuerza de atracción o repulsión generadas por cargas eléctricas en movimiento o que giran (41)

magnetic pole/polo magnético uno de dos puntos, tales como los extremos de un imán, que tienen cualidades magnéticas opuestas (40)

microprocessor/microprocesador un chip único de un semiconductor, el cual controla y ejecuta las instrucciones de una microcomputadora (85)

P

parallel circuit/circuito paralelo un circuito en el que las partes están unidas en ramas de manera tal que la diferencia de potencial entre cada parte es la misma (27)

photocell/fotocelda un aparato que transforma la energía luminosa en energía eléctrica (18)

R

resistance/resistencia en ciencias físicas, la oposición que un material o aparato presenta a la corriente (15)

S

semiconductor/semiconductor un elemento o compuesto que conduce la corriente eléctrica mejor que un aislante, pero no tan bien como un conductor (71)

series circuit/circuito en serie un circuito en el que las partes están unidas una después de la otra de manera tal que la corriente en cada parte es la misma (26)

software/software un conjunto de instrucciones o comandos que le dicen qué hacer a una computadora; un programa de computadora (89)

solenoid/solenoide una bobina de alambre que tiene una corriente eléctrica (49)

static electricity/electricidad estática carga eléctrica en reposo; por lo general se produce por fricción o inducción (8)

T

thermocouple/termopar un aparato que transforma la energía térmica en energía eléctrica (18)

transformer/transformador un aparato que aumenta o disminuye el voltaje de la corriente alterna (58)

V

voltage/voltaje la diferencia de potencial entre dos puntos, medida en voltios (14)

Index

Boldface page numbers refer to illustrative material, such as figures, tables, margin elements, photographs, and illustrations.

A

AC (alternating current), 13, **13**
  diodes and, 72
  generators of, 57, **57**
  voltage of, 15
acceleration, 128, 130
alarm clocks, **84**
alnico, 44
alternating current (AC), 13, **13**
  diodes and, 72
  generators of, 57, **57**
  voltage of, 15
ammeters, 30–31
Ampère, André-Marie, 49
amperes (A), 12
amplifiers, transistors in, 73, **73**
analog recording, 78, **78**
analog signals, 77–78, **77, 80**
animal compasses, **42**
antennas, **80**
Archimedes' principle, 129
area, **116**, 127
armatures, 52, **52,** 60
arsenic, **71**
atoms
  in domains, 42, **43**
  electric force and electric fields in, 5
  law of electric charges in, 4, **4, 5**
  magnetism and, 42
auroras, 46, **46**
average acceleration, 130
averages, 124
average speed, 130

B

balances, triple-beam, 118
bar graphs, 123, **123**
batteries, 14, **14**
Bernoulli's principle, 130
binary numbers, 78
body temperature, **117**
Boyle's law, 129
Bradbury, Ray, 98
brushes, **56**
buoyant force, 129
burglar alarms, 26

C

carriers, 76
cars
  jumper cables for, 8, **8**
  remote controlled toy, 74, **74**
  voltages in, 14, **14**
catalysts
CD-R (CD-recordable), 88, **88**
CD-RW (CD-rewritable), 88, **88**
CDs (compact discs), 78–79, **78, 79,** 88, **88**
cells, electrical, 17–18, **17, 18**
Celsius scale, **117**
central processing units (CPUs), 86, **86**
charge, electric
  charging objects, 6–7, **6, 7**
  conservation of, 7
  detection of, 7, **7**
  lab on, **7**
  law of electric charges, 4, **5**
  moving charges, 8, **8**
  static electricity, 8–10
Charles's law, 129
charts, 121–123, **121, 122, 123**
circle graphs, 121, **121**
circuit boards, 70, **70**
circuit breakers, 28, **28**
circuits, electric, 24–29
  integrated, 74, **74**
  labs on, **26–27,** 30–31
  parts of, 24–25, **24, 25**
  safety tips and, 28–29, **28, 29**
  switches in, 25, **25**
  types of, 25–27, **26, 27,** 30–31
CME (coronal mass ejections), 66
coils, wire, **56, 57**
color television, 81–82, **81, 82**
communication technology, 76–83
  analog signals, 77–78, **77, 78**
  digital signals, 78–79, **78, 79**
  labs on, **85,** 92–93
  Morse code, 76, **76,** 92–93
  plasma displays, 82, **82**
  radios, 75, **75,** 80, **80**
  television, 70, 81–82, **81, 82**
commutators, 52, **52,** 60
compact discs (CDs), 78–79, **78, 79,** 88, **88**
compasses
  animals as, **42**
  Earth and, 45–46, **45**
  electric currents and, 48, **48**
  north and south poles of, 41, **41**
computers, 84–91, **85**
  basic functions of, 84, **84**
  binary digits in, 78
  burning and erasing CDs using, 88, **88**
  hardware, 86–87, **86, 87**
  history of, 85, **85, 86**
  lab on, **85**
  networks, 90, **90**
  software, 89, **89**
  technicians, 99
  wearable, 98
computer technicians, 99
concentration, 131
conclusions, 120
conductivity, electrical
  charging by conduction, 6, **6**
  of conductors, 8, **8**
  resistance and, 15
  of semiconductors, 71, **71**
  temperature and, 16
conductors, electric, 8, **8.** See also conductivity, electrical
conservation of energy, law of, 128
control groups, 120
controlled experiments, 120
conversions, unit, **116, 117**
copper, 15
coronal mass ejections (CMEs), 66
CPUs (central processing units), 86, **86**
cross-multiplication, 124
cube volume, 127
cubic centimeters, **116**
cubic meters, **116**
current, electric, 12, **12**
  alternating current, 13, **13,** 15, 57, 72
  diodes and, 72, **72**
  direct current, 13, **13,** 72
  discovery of electromagnetism, 48–49, **48**
  electrical cells, 17–18, **17, 18**
  induction by magnetism, 54–56, **54, 55, 56**
  magnetic force and, 51, **51**
  measurement by galvanometers, 53
  Ohm's law, 20, **20**
  resistance and, 15–16, **16**
  in series and parallel circuits, 25–27, **26, 27,** 30–31
  solenoids and, 49, **49**
  voltage and, 14–15, **14**

D

data, 122, **122**
DC (direct current), 13, **13,** 72
DC electric motors, 52, **52,** 60–61
decimals, 125

Index

density, 131
dependent variables, 122, **122**
digital recording, 79, **79**
digital signals, 78–79, **78, 79,** 81
diodes, 72, **72**
direct current (DC), 13, **13,** 72
direct current electric motors, 52,
   52, 60–61
domains, 42, **43**
doorbells, 51, **51**
doping, 71, **71**
dry cells, 17

E

Earth, 45–46, **45, 46**
earthquakes, **77**
electrical calculations, 20–23
electrical cells, 17–18, **17, 18**
electrical conductivity
   charging by conduction, 6, **6**
   conductors, 8, **8**
   resistance and, **15**
   of semiconductors, 71, **71**
   temperature and, 16
electrical conductors, 8, **8.** *See also*
   electrical conductivity
electrical current, 12–19. *See also*
   electric current
electrical energy, 12–19
   generating, 17–18, **17, 18,** 57, **57**
   measuring, 22, **22,** 30–31
electrical insulators, 8, **8**
electrical outlets, 15
electric charge, 4–11
   charging objects, 6–7, **6, 7**
   conservation of, 7
   detection of, 7, **7**
   lab on, **7**
   law of electric charges, 4
   moving charges, 8, **8**
   in static electricity, 8–10
electric circuits, 24–29
   integrated, 74, **74**
   labs on, **27,** 30–31
   parts of, 24–25, **24, 25**
   safety tips, 28–29, **28, 29**
   switches in, 25, **25**
   types of, 25–27, **26, 27,** 30–31
electric current, 12, **12**
   alternating current, 13, **13,** 15,
      57, 72
   diodes and, 72, **72**
   direct current, 13, **13,** 72
   discovery of electromagnetism,
      48–49, **48**
   electrical cells, 17–18, **17, 18**
   induction by magnetism, 54–56,
      54, 55, 56
   magnetic force and, 51, **51**

measurement by galvanometers,
   53
Ohm's law, 20, **20**
resistance and, 15–16, **16**
in series and parallel circuits,
   25–27, **26, 27,** 30–31
solenoids and, 49, **49**
voltage and, 14–15, **14**
electric discharges, 9–10, **9, 10,** 36
electric eels, **15,** 36
electric fields, 5, **5**
electric force, 5, **5**
electric generators, 56–57, **56, 57**
electricians, 37
electricity, 4–29. *See also* electric
   current; electromagnetism
   electrical cells, 17–18, **17, 18**
   electric charge, 4–8, **6, 7**
   electric circuits, 24–29, **24, 25,**
      26, 27
   electric power, 21–22
   generators, 56–57, **56, 57**
   magnetism and, 48–59
   measuring, 22–23, **22,** 30–31
   nervous impulses, **25**
   Ohm's law, 20, **21,** 30–31
   resistance, 15–16, **15, 16,** 20, **20**
   safety tips, 28–29, **28, 29**
   static, 8–10, **9, 10**
   switches, 25, **25**
   transformers, 58, **58, 59**
   voltage, 14–15
   ways to save, 23, **23**
electric meters, 22, **22**
electric motors, 52, **52,** 60–61
electric power, 21, **21**
electrodes, 17, **17**
electrolytes, 17
electromagnetic force, 41, **41**
electromagnetic induction, 54–56,
   54, 55, 56
electromagnetic waves (EM waves),
   in radios, 80, **80.** *See also*
   sound waves
electromagnetism, 38–59, **49**
   applications of, 51–53, **51, 52,**
      66
   auroras and, 46, **46**
   discovery of, 48, **48**
   Earth as a magnet, 45–46, **45**
   electric generators, 56–57, **56, 57**
   electric motors, 52, **52,** 60–61
   electromagnets, 44, 50, **50**
   induction of electric current,
      54–56, **54, 55, 56**
   labs on, **50,** 60–61
   losing alignment, 43
   maglev trains, 48, 50
   magnet cutting, 44, **44**
   magnetic fields, 42, **42, 43,** 45,
      45

magnetic force, 41, **41,** 51, **51**
magnet making, 43, **43**
magnet properties, 40–41, **40,**
   41
   in record players, 78, **78**
   solenoids, 49, **49**
   transformers, 58, **58, 59**
electromagnets, 44, 50, **50**
electronic devices, 70–75
electronic technology, 70–91
   analog signals, 77–78, **77, 78**
   circuit boards, 70, **70**
   computers, 84–90, **84, 86, 88,**
      90
   digital signals, 78–79, **78, 79**
   diodes, 72, **72**
   integrated circuits, 74, **74**
   labs on, **85,** 92–92
   plasma displays, 82, **82**
   semiconductors, 71, **71**
   transistors, 73–74, **73, 74,** 85
   vacuum tubes and, 75, **75**
electrons
   in diodes, 72, **72**
   in electric current, 12–13, **13**
   magnetic fields, 42
   in semiconductors, 71, **71**
   in televisions, 81, **81**
electroscopes, 7, **7**
elves, 36
EM waves (electromagnetic waves),
   in radios, 80, **80.** *See also*
   sound waves
energy, electrical, 12–19
   generating, 17–18, **17, 18,** 57, **57**
   measuring, 22, **22,** 30–31
English units, **116**
ENIAC computer, 85, **85, 86**
experimental groups, 120
experiments, controlled, 120

F

Fahrenheit scale, **117**
families (groups), **132–133**
Faraday, Michael, 54–55, **54,** 67
ferromagnets, 44, **44**
fields, electric, 5, **5.** *See also* magnetic fields
fluids, Pascal's principle in, 129
fluorescent materials, **81, 82**
FoldNote instructions, 110–113,
   110, 111, 112, 113
forces
   electric, 5, **5**
   electromagnetic, 41, **41**
   magnetic, 41, **41**
   net, 130
fractions, 125–126
Franklin, Benjamin, **10**

Index

freezing points, **117**
friction, charging objects by, 6, **6**
fuses, 28, **28**

G

gallium, **71**
galvanometers, 53
GCF (greatest common factor), 125
generators, electric, 56–57, **56, 57**
geomagnetic storms, 66
GFCIs (ground fault circuit inter-
        rupters), 28, **28**
gigabytes, **87**
Gilbert, William, 45
graduated cylinders, 118
grams, **116**
Graphic Organizer instructions,
        114–115, **114, 115**
graphs
        bar, 123, **123**
        circle, 121, **121**
        line, 122–123, **122**
        slopes of, 122–123
gravitation, law of universal, 128
greatest common factor (GCF), 125
ground fault circuit interrupters
        (GFCIs), 28, **28**
grounding, 10, **10**
groups, **132–133**

H

hardware, computer, 86–87, **86, 87**
hectares, **116**
Henry, Joseph, 54
hydroelectric power plants, 57, **57**
hypotheses, 119–120

I

independent variables, 122, **122**
induction
        by changing magnetic fields,
                54–56, **54, 55, 56**
        charging objects by, **6,** 7
inertia, 128
input, computer, 84, **84,** 86, **86**
input devices, 86, **86**
insulators, electrical, 8, **8**
integrated circuits, 74, **74**
interface cards, 87
International System of Units (SI),
        116
Internet, 90, **90**
Internet Service Providers (ISPs),
        90, **90**
iron, 44, **44**

J

jumper cables, 8, **8**

K

kelvins, 117
Kelvin scale, **117**
kilobytes, **87**
kilograms (kg), **116**
kilowatt-hours (kWh), 22, **22**
kilowatts (kW), 21

L

LANs (Local Area Networks), 90, **90**
lasers, in CD players, 79, **79**
law of conservation of energy, 128
law of electric charges, 4, **5**
law of reflection, 129
law of universal gravitation, 128
laws, scientific, 128–130
laws of motion, Newton's, 128
least common denominator (LCD),
        126
LED (light-emitting diodes), 70
length, **116,** 118, **118**
light bulbs, 21, **21,** 26, **26**
light-emitting diodes (LED), 70
lightning, 9–10, **9, 10,** 36
lightning rods, 10, **10**
linear relationships, 122
line graphs, 122, **122**
liquids, volume measurements of,
        118
liters, **116**
loads, electrical, 24–25, **24**
Local Area Networks (LANs), 90, **90**
lodestone (magnetite), 40, 44, **44,
        46**
longitudinal waves. *See* sound
        waves

M

maglev trains, 48, 50
magnetic field lines, **42**
magnetic fields
        around the Earth, 45–46, **45**
        changing domains with, **43**
        field lines, 42, **42**
        induction of current from, 54–
                56, **54, 55, 56**
        from solenoids, 49–50, **49**

magnetic force, 41, **41**
magnetic levitation trains, 48, 50
magnetic poles, 40, **40**
        on Earth, 45, **45**
        north and south, 41, **41**
magnetic resonance imaging (MRI),
        66
magnetism, 40–47. *See also*
        magnets
        cause of, 42–44
        of Earth, 45–46, **45**
        electric current and, 51, **51,** 54,
                54
        labs on, **45,** 60–61
        loss of alignment, 43
        magnetic forces, 41, **41**
        making magnets, 43, **43**
        medical uses, 66
        superconductors and, **16**
magnetite, 40, 44, **44, 46**
magnets, 40–47, **40**
        cutting, 44, **44**
        Earth as, 45–46, **45**
        electromagnets, 44, 50, **50**
        in galvanometers, 53
        kinds of, 44
        losing magnetism, 43
        magnetic fields, 42, **42, 43,**
                45–46, **45**
        making, 43, **43,** 60–61
        north and south poles, 40–41,
                41, 44–45, **44, 45**
        properties of, 40–41, **40, 41**
        solenoids as, 49, **49**
mass, **116,** 118
mass numbers, **132–133**
math refresher, 124–127
Maxwell, James Clerk, 67
means, 124
measurements
        of current, 53
        of electrical energy, 22, **22,**
                30–31
        of length, 118, **118**
        of liquid volume, 118
        of mass and weight, 118
memory, computer, 87, **87**
metalloids, **132–133**
metals, **132–133**
meters, **116**
metersticks, 118, **118**
metric rulers, 118, **118**
metric system, 116, **116**
microphones, 73, **73, 80**
microprocessors, 85, **85**
milliliters, **116**
modems, 87
modulators, **80**
Morse code, 76, **76,** 92–93
motors, electric, 52, **52,** 60–61
MRI (magnetic resonance imaging),
        66

Index

N

nervous impulses, **25**
net force, 130
networks, computer, 90, **90**
Newton's laws of motion, 128
nonlinear relationships, 122
nonmetals, **132–133**
northern lights, 46, **46**
north pole, in magnets, 41, **41**, 45, **45**
n-type semiconductors, **71**, 72–73, **72**, **73**
nuclear power plants, 57

O

Oersted, Hans Christian, 48–49, **48**, 54
Ohm, Georg, **21**
Ohm's law, 20, **21**, 30–31
outlets, electrical, 15
output, computer, 84, **84**
output devices, 87

P

paint colors, 75–77
parallel circuits, 27, **27**, 30–31
Pascal's principle, 129
percentages, 125
Perez, Pete, 37
periodic table, **132–133**
periods, **132–133**
permanent magnets, 44, **56**
phonograph records, 78, **78**
photocells, 18, **18**
plasma display, 82, **82**
power, 21, **21**, 131
power plants, 57, **57**
prefixes, in SI units, **116**
pressure, 129, 131
prisms, 127
processing, computer, 84, **84**
proportions, 124
p-type semiconductors, **71**, 72–73, **72**, **73**

R

radios, 75, **75**, 80, **80**
radio waves, 80, **80**
RAM (random-access memory), 87
ratios, 124
read-only memory (ROM), 87
records, phonograph, 78, **78**
rectangle, area of a, 127
reflection, law of, 129
remote controls, 70, **70**

resistance, 15–16, **15**, **16**, 20, **20**
Riley, Agnes, 99
ROM (read-only memory), 87

S

safety tips on electric circuits, 28–29, **28**, **29**
scientific laws, 128–130
scientific methods, 119–120
scientific notation, 127
seismograms, **77**
seismographs, **77**
semiconductors, 71, **71**
    doping, 71, **71**
    n-type, **71**, 72–73, **72**, **73**
    p-type, **71**, 72–73, **72**, **73**
series circuits, 26, **26**, 30–31
shocks, electric, 9, 28, **28**
signals, 76, 77, **77**, 92–93
silicon, 71, **71**
SI units, **116**
slopes, of graphs, 122–123
software, computer, 89, **89**
solar panels, 18
solar winds, 66
solenoids, 49–51, **49**, **50**, **51**
sound waves
    amplifiers and, 73, **73**
    in CDs, 79, **79**
    in radios, **80**
    telephones and, 77, **77**
southern lights, 46, **46**
south pole, in magnets, 41, **41**, 45, **45**
speed, **85**, 130
sprites, 36
square, area of a, 127
static electricity, 4–11, **8**, **9**, **10**
step-up/step-down transformers, 58, **58**, **59**
storage, computer, 84, **84**
stylus, 78, **78**
sun, geomagnetic storms and, 66
superconductors, 16, **16**
switches, 25, **25**, 74, **74**

T

telegraphs, 76, **76**, 92–93
telephones, analog signals in, 77, **77**
television
    images on, 81, **81**
    plasma displays, 82, **82**
    remote controls, 70, **70**
temperature
    electrical resistance and, 16, **16**
    magnetism and, 43

temperature scales, **117**
    unit conversions, **117**
temperature scales, **117**
temporary magnets, 44
"There Will Come Soft Rains," 98
thermocouples, 18, **18**
thunderstorms, 9–10, **9**, **10**, 36
transformers, 58, **58**, **59**
transistors, 73–74, **73**, **74**, 85
triangle, area of a, 127
triple-beam balances, 118
turbines, 57, **57**

U

units
    of electric current, 12
    of household energy use, 22, **22**
    of power, 21
    prefixes, **116**
    SI conversion table, **116**
    of volume, **116**
    of work, 131
universal gravitation, law of, 128

V

vacuum tubes, 75, **75**, 85
variables, 120, 122
vinyl records, 78, **78**
voltage, 14, **14**
    from electric eels, **15**, 36
    energy and, 14
    measuring, 30–31
    Ohm's law, 20, **20**
    in parallel circuits, 27
    transformers and, 58, **58**, **59**
    varying, **14**, 15
voltmeters, 30–31
volume
    of cubes, 127
    formulas for, 127
    of a gas, 129
    of liquids, 118
    units of, **116**

W

water, freezing point of, **117**
watts (W), 21
wearable computers, 98
wet cells, 17, **17**
wires, **24**
work, 131
working memory, 87
World Wide Web, 90

Credits

Abbreviations used: (t) top, (c) center, (b) bottom, (l) left, (r) right, (bkgd) background

PHOTOGRAPHY

Front Cover Robert Essel/Corbis

Skills Practice Lab Teens Sam Dudgeon/HRW

Connection to Astrology Corbis Images; **Connection to Biology** David M. Phillips/Visuals Unlimited; **Connection to Chemistry** Digital Image copyright © 2005 PhotoDisc; **Connection to Environment** Digital Image copyright © 2005 PhotoDisc; **Connection to Geology** Letraset Phototone; **Connection to Language Arts** Digital Image copyright © 2005 PhotoDisc; **Connection to Meteorology** Digital Image copyright © 2005 PhotoDisc; **Connection to Oceanography** © ICONOTEC; **Connection to Physics** Digital Image copyright © 2005 PhotoDisc

Table of Contents iv (cl), John Langford/HRW; iv (b), ©National Geographic Image Collection/Richard T. Nowitz; v (tl), Sam Dudgeon/HRW; v (tr), © Reuters NewMedia Inc./CORBIS; vi–vii, Victoria Smith/HRW; x (bl), Sam Dudgeon/HRW; xi (tl), John Langford/HRW; xi (b), Sam Dudgeon/HRW; xii (tl), Victoria Smith/HRW; xii (bl), Stephanie Morris/HRW; xii (br), Sam Dudgeon/HRW; xiii (tl), Patti Murray/Animals, Animals; xiii (tr), Jana Birchum/HRW; xiii (b), Peter Van Steen/HRW

Chapter One 2–3 (all), Courtesy Sandia National Laboratories; 6 (bc), John Langford/HRW; 6 (bl), Sam Dudgeon/HRW; 7 (tr), John Langford/HRW; 8 (tl), © COMSTOCK, Inc.; 10 (br), Paul Katz/Index Stock Imagery/PictureQuest; 481 (cr), Michelle Bridwell/HRW; 11 (tr), Sam Dudgeon/HRW; 14 (br), Sam Dudgeon/HRW; 15 (tl), © National Geographic Image Collection/Richard T. Nowitz; 16 (br), Takeshi Takahara/Photo Researchers, Inc.; 17 (br), John Langford/HRW; 19 (tr), John Langford/HRW; 21 (br), Sam Dudgeon/HRW; 22 (tl, tc), Sam Dudgeon/HRW; 23 (cl), Digital Image copyright © 2005 PhotoDisc; 23 (c), © Brand X Pictures; 24 (bl), Richard T. Nowitz/Photo Researchers, Inc.; 24 (bc, br, inset), Sam Dudgeon/HRW; 25 (all), John Langford/HRW; 26 (b), John Langford/HRW; 27 (b), Sam Dudgeon/HRW; 28 (tl), Paul Silverman/Fundamental Photographs; 28 (bc), Sam Dudgeon/HRW; 29 (all), Sam Dudgeon/HRW; 30 (bl), John Langford/HRW; 31 (b), Victoria Smith/HRW; 32 (br), Sam Dudgeon/HRW; 33 (br), John Langford/HRW; 33 (tl), © COMSTOCK, Inc.; 36 (tr), Daniel L. Osborne, University of Alaska/Detlev Ban Ravenswaay/Science Photo Library/Photo Researchers, Inc.; 36 (tl), Sonia S. Wasco/Grant Heilman Photography, Inc.; 36 (cr), STARLab, Stanford University; 37 (cr), Sam Dudgeon/HRW

Chapter Two 38–39 (all), © NASA/Photo Researchers, Inc.; 40 (bc), Sam Dudgeon/HRW; 41 (tr, bc, br), Richard Megna/Fundamental Photographs; 41 (cr), Sam Dudgeon/HRW; 42 (tr), Richard Megna/Fundamental Photographs; 43 (br), Sam Dudgeon/HRW; 44 (cl), Sam Dudgeon/HRW; 46 (br), Pekka Parviainen/Science Photo Library/Photo Researchers, Inc.; 47 (tr), Sam Dudgeon/HRW; 50 (br), © Tom Tracy/The Stock Shop; 51 (tr), Victoria Smith/HRW; 53 (cr), Gamma Photo/Central Scientific Company; 53 (tr), Sam Dudgeon/HRW; 60 (cr), Sam Dudgeon/HRW; 61 (bl), David Young Wolf/PhotoEdit; 62 (tl), Sam Dudgeon/HRW; 66 (cl), © Getty Images; 66 (tr), Howard Sochurek; 67 (tr), © Baldwin Ward/CORBIS

Chapter Three 68–69 (all), © Peter Menzel Photography; 70 (all), Sam Dudgeon/HRW; 72 (tl), Sam Dudgeon/HRW; 73 (tr), Sam Dudgeon/HRW; 74 (bl), Sam Dudgeon/HRW; 75 (all), Sam Dudgeon/HRW; 76 (bl), Digital Image copyright © 2005 PhotoDisc; 78 (bl), Digital Image copyright © 2005 PhotoDisc; 81 (inset), Corbis Images; 82 (inset), Corbis Images; 84 (br), Sam Dudgeon/HRW; 85 (tr), Corbis–Bettmann; 86 (b), Sam Dudgeon/HRW; 87 (b), Sam Dudgeon/HRW; 91 (all), Sam Dudgeon/HRW; 92 (bl), Sam Dudgeon/HRW; 93 (b), Sam Dudgeon/HRW; 94 (br), Sam Dudgeon/HRW; 95 (bl), Sam Dudgeon/HRW; 98 (tl), © Reuters NewMedia Inc./CORBIS; 99 (cr), Courtesy Agnes Riley; 99 (bl), Digital Image copyright © 2005 PhotoDisc

Lab Book/Appendix "LabBook Header", "L", Corbis Images; "a", Letraset Phototone; "b", and "B", HRW; "o", and "k", images ©2006 PhotoDisc/HRW; 100 (cr), Sam Dudgeon/HRW; 102 (br), Sam Dudgeon/HRW; 103 (b), Sam Dudgeon/HRW; 104 (b), Sam Dudgeon/HRW; 105 (all), Sam Dudgeon/HRW; 106 (b), Sam Dudgeon/HRW; 107 (b), Sam Dudgeon/HRW; 111 (br), Victoria Smith; 112 (br), Victoria Smith; 118 (tr), Peter Van Steen/HRW; 118 (br), Sam Dudgeon/HRW; 130 (tr), Sam Dudgeon/HRW